Pedagogy
of Solidarity

Qualitative Inquiry and Social Justice

Series editors

Norman K. Denzin
University of Illinois, Champaign-Urbana

Yvonna S. Lincoln
Texas A&M University

Books in this series address the role of critical qualitative research in an era that cries out for emancipatory visions that move people to struggle and resist oppression. Rooted in an ethical framework that is based on human rights and social justice, the series publishes exemplary studies that advance this transformative paradigm.

Volumes in this series

Volume 4. **Pedagogy of Solidarity**
Paulo Freire, Ana Maria Araújo Freire, and Walter de Oliveira

Volume 3. **Ethnotheatre: Research from Page to Stage**
Johnny Saldaña

Volume 2. **Body, Paper, Stage: Writing and Performing Autoethnography**
Tami Spry

Volume 1. **Betweener Talk: Decolonizing Knowledge Production, Pedagogy, and Praxis**
Marcelo Diversi and Cláudio Moreira

Pedagogy of Solidarity

Paulo Freire
Patron of Brazilian Education

Ana Maria Araújo Freire
Walter de Oliveira

Routledge
Taylor & Francis Group

LONDON AND NEW YORK

First published 2014 by Left Coast Press, Inc.

Published 2016 by Routledge
2 Park Square, Milton Park, Abingdon, Oxon OX14 4RN
711 Third Avenue, New York, NY 10017, USA

Routledge is an imprint of the Taylor & Francis Group, an informa business

Library of Congress Cataloging-in-Publication Data

Freire, Paulo, 1921-1997.
 Pedagogy of solidarity / Paulo Freire, patron of Brazilian education, Ana
Maria Araújo Freire, Walter de Oliveira ; foreword by Henry A Giroux.
 pages   cm.— (Qualitative inquiry & social justice ; 4)
Summary: "Famous Brazilian educational and social theorist Paulo Freire presents his ideas on the importance of community solidarity in moving toward social justice in schools and society. In a set of talks and interviews shortly before his death, Freire addresses issues not often highlighted in his work, such as globalization, post-modern fatalism, and the qualities of educators for the 21st century. His illuminating comments are supplemented with commentaries by other well-known scholars, such as Ana Maria Araújo Freire, Norman Denzin, Henry Giroux, and Donaldo Macedo"— Provided by publisher.
 Includes bibliographical references and index.
ISBN 978-1-61132-964-3 (hardback) — ISBN 978-1-61132-965-0 (paperback) — ISBN 978-1-61132-966-7 (institutional ebook) — ISBN 978-1-61132-967-4 (consumer eBook)
 1. Critical pedagogy. 2. Popular education. 3. Community and school. I. Freire, Ana Maria Araújo, 1933– II. Oliveira, Walter Ferreira de. III. Title.
LC196.F738 2014
370.115—dc23
 2013044334

ISBN 978-1-61132-964-3 hardcover
ISBN 978-1-61132-965-0 paperback

Copyediting: Susan Walters Schmid, Teton Editorial
Design and Production: Detta Penna
Indexing: Kirsten Kite

Contents

Memory's Hope
In the Shadow of
Paulo Freire's Presence

Henry A. Giroux

Paulo Freire tells a story in one of the chapters in this book about being asked by someone "What can we do in order to follow you?" Paulo, in typical form, answers "If you follow me, you destroy me. The best way for you to understand me is to reinvent me and not to try to become adapted to me." Paulo had little patience with education as either a form of training, method, or as a political and moral practice that closed down history, the potential of individual and social agency, the joy and importance of engaged solidarity, the importance of social responsibility, and the possibility of hope. Paulo was a critical intellectual who was prescient because he took risks, took positions without standing still, and strongly argued that education was not merely the foundation of learning but a prerequisite for critically reading the world and transforming that world with the aim of making it better. Paulo was incredibly insightful in creating dialectical webs that connected seemingly unrelated practices. When he talked about the relationship between authority and freedom, he not only engaged the issue of the limits and possibilities of freedom in a democratic society, he also focused on *how* such a dialectic worked itself out in the theory and practice of the classroom. When he talked about all human activity beginning with history, he not only grounded his understanding of the unfinished human

Pedagogy of Solidarity, Paulo Freire, Ana Maria Araújo Freire, and Walter de Oliveira. © 2014 by Ana Maria Araújo Freire and Walter Ferreira de Oliveira, pp. 7-12.

being in a logic of self-determination and hope, he also talked about the importance of intellectual curiosity in the classroom and how it and a culture of questioning were central to a pedagogy of the unfinished. When he wrote about social justice and our responsibility to others as part of a broader discourse of global democracy, he also made clear how justice and responsibility were central to honouring the experiences, voices, and beliefs that students bring to the classroom, and how important it was to not only affirm such voices, but also to fulfill our responsibility as teachers to enable them to become more than they were, to expand the knowledge they brought to the classroom, and to broaden their sense of community and solidarity beyond their family, village, neighbourhood, and even nation. Paulo was a worldly intellectual who never allowed himself to forget the connection between the abstract and the everyday, the global and the local, the self and the other. His ongoing interrogations over the ever-changing relationship between determinism and hope, privatization and solidarity, training and critical learning, conversation and substantive dialogue, and freedom and authority are as crucial today as they were during the many years in which addressed them in numerous talks, articles, and books. Right up to his untimely death, he was more concerned about asking better questions than providing answers or offering his readers what some have called methodologies. Freire was an intellectual who turned his own exile into a matter of destiny rather than fate, from a misfortune into an opportunity to become an intellectual who was worldly and spoke to a global audience. Transforming fate into destiny was central to Freire's understanding of what it meant to be human and to his comprehension of the intellectual as a crucial social, cultural, and ethical critic, and how both were integral to his own life and work.

Before his death, Paulo was well aware of the growing authoritarianism that was emerging in many Western countries. Militarism was on the rise as were new attacks on immigrants. Liberal capitalism was being transformed into a virulent form of market fundamentalism dominated by the irrational belief that markets could solve all problems. There was also the dismantling of the social state, the ongoing criminalization of social problems, and the massive disinvestment and dismantling of public education by corporations and neoliberal warriors. And there was also the concerted attempt on the part of governments to manufacture cynicism in the form of end of history arguments, while normalizing oppressive relations of economic, cultural, and social violence. The culture of fear that Paulo had personally experienced in Brazil had in a post–9/11 world become a matter of state policy in many countries, especially in the United States. Torture and abduction were now condoned in countries that once claimed they were the citadels of freedom and human rights. Since Paulo's death we have entered a period that Hannah Arendt once called "dark times." While there are many themes in Paulo's work that need to be reclaimed as part of the current struggle to link education to the promise of a global and inclusive democracy, I want to focus primarily on his notion of hope, because the narcotic public pedagogy of neoliberalism with its altering of history, its erasure of social struggles, its incessant attack on the public sphere, and its utterly privatized and consumerist view of agency has made educated hope seem out of date, a luxury for another age. Of course, there can be no democratic politics without hope, just as their can be no critical teachers without hope, nor any curious students or culture of questioning without hope. The discourse of critique and possibility, hope at a time of hopelessness, runs through every aspect of Paulo's pedagogy and critical and expansive philosophy.

Hope in the Age of Disposability

Freire's belief in the ability of people to resist and transform the weight of oppressive institutions and ideologies has been forged in a spirit of struggle tempered by both the grim realities of his own imprisonment and exile and a profound sense of humility, compassion, and hope. Acutely aware that many contemporary versions of hope were not anchored in practice and lacked a historical concreteness, Freire repeatedly denounced such romantic fantasies and has been passionate about recovering and rearticulating hope through, in his words, an "understanding of history as opportunity and not determinism."[1] Hope for Freire is a practice of witnessing, an act of moral imagination that encourages progressive educators and others to stand at the edge of society, to think beyond existing configurations of power in order to imagine the unthinkable in terms of how they might live with dignity, justice, and freedom. Hope demands an anchoring in transformative practices, and one of the tasks of the progressive educator is to "unveil opportunities for hope, no matter what the obstacles may be."[2] Freire's notion of hope is grounded in a celebration of human agency and a full-scale attack on the fear of freedom. Not only freedom from oppressive authority but freedom in those forms of state authority that create the conditions for overcoming necessity, human suffering, poverty, lack of education, and those varied social problems that turn freedom into curse strangled by mere struggle to survive on a daily basis. Freedom for Freire meant not only individual freedom, but also the freedom to participate with others in shaping those forces that bear down on our lives. But, such freedom and the education needed to give it meaning became impossible in the face of widespread cynicism and unrelenting hopelessness. At a time when death inhabited so strongly the presumption that the future was merely a repeat of the present, Freire fought courageously for the idea that there was no possibility for humanity without an undying hope and belief in the possibility of struggle and change. Freire refused to take emancipation off the agenda and at the same time believed there were no short cuts to such a challenge.

Underlying Freire's politics of hope is a view of pedagogy that locates itself on the dividing lines where the relations between domination and oppression, power and powerlessness continue to be produced and reproduced. Understanding that the first task of dominant politics is to make power invisible, Freire argued for intellectuals to take on the responsibility to make the mechanisms of power visible at every level of social interaction and to do so through a self-conscious project of making students and others aware of the mechanisms that render life painful and needless human suffering acceptable. And yet, for Paulo, intellectuals were not to assume the role of legislators or impotent martinets pushing some party line. On the contrary, intellectuals had to take a stand without becoming doctrinaire, dedicate their lives to study of social problems, assume some responsibility for making public connections and addressing the causes of human suffering. Paulo in this sense was not dispassionate, disinterested, or simply a mechanical intellectual who hid behind the cloak of objectivity or indulged the neutral language of training. He was someone who modeled hope as a thoughtful and critical activism; hope in this case represented both a referent for imagining a different future and a pedagogical encounter and willingness to act otherwise. History for Paulo was the foundation on which human agency developed, but it was not a ground to be revered. On the contrary, it was a belief in the redemption of the hopes of the past, rather than in a mindless reverence for it that animated Freire's belief in history and the unfinished quality of what it meant to be human. For Freire, the struggle for reclaiming a pedagogy of hope and struggle must be connected to the best that democracy can offer, which means recognizing that a society never reaches the limits of justice and should assume the collective responsibility of putting into place the material and symbolic resources that constitute "the means of dignifying people so they become fully free to claim their moral and political agency."[3]

The chapters that make up this book emerge from a past that is no longer with us, but at the same time they speak to a present that offers important possibilities for a different kind of future. Paulo's generosity, his fierceness of spirit, his faith in human beings, and his belief in education as the foundation for action and agency over the dismal demands of necessity are crucial to any understanding of the challenges we now face at this dark time in history. In Paulo's lived experiences we saw an amazing affirmation of human solidarity, while in his words we are comforted with the possibility of making such solidarity not merely a cherished memory but part of a beloved community.

Notes

1. Paulo Freire, *Pedagogy of Hope* (New York: Continuum Press, 1994), 91.
2. Ibid., 9.
3. Bill Moyers, "A Time for Anger, A Call to Action," *Common Dreams* (February 7, 2007), http://www.commondreams.org/views07/0322-24.htm.

Chapter 1

Introduction to Pedagogy of Solidarity

Walter Ferreira de Oliveira

In opening the conference given by Paulo Freire at the University of Northern Iowa in 1996, the university's president, Dr. Robert Koob, noted that it is a very important moment in our lives when we have an opportunity to rub shoulders with greatness. He likened his feelings to those of many years before in the 1960s when he had heard Dr. Martin Luther King speak in a nearby university hall, brilliantly discussing the most relevant issues of the day. Paulo Freire was in a similar category, recognized at the University of Northern Iowa as one of the most distinguished scholars of the twentieth century and an educator of great impact throughout the whole world. His impact transcends the specific domain of literacy and reaches to all aspects of the field of education in all parts of the planet. His philosophical teachings have helped to change our understanding, not only about education but about the human condition itself. Schools and universities would not be the same without his influence.

It is therefore not an easy task to introduce another part of the legacy of Paulo Freire, the *Pedagogy of Solidarity*, here enriched with commentary by renowned authors such as Henry Giroux, Donaldo Macedo, and Norman K. Denzin, paired with the contributions of Nita Freire and

Pedagogy of Solidarity, Paulo Freire, Ana
Maria Araújo Freire, and Walter de Oliveira.
© 2014 by Ana Maria Araújo Freire and
Walter Ferreira de Oliveira, pp. 13–14.

myself. Having been born in Brazil, my life has been deeply affected as a student, as a professional, and as an educator by the ideas, philosophy, and teachings of Freire. His name is synonymous with liberation, freedom, struggle against oppression, hope, and pedagogy in its ultimate meaning.

Education, which is one of the most important forms of socialization, has been fundamentally changed throughout the world due to Paulo Freire's influence. His seminal works, such as *Pedagogy of Hope,* which represents a revisiting of his *Pedagogy of the Oppressed*, and *Pedagogy of Autonomy*, allow us to penetrate the realm of education in a particular way, and realize its inextricable links with the systems of oppression. A number of other publications since then have also emphasized that educators can, and must, be broadcasters of hope and not accomplices of despair. The institution of education begins with struggle and is kept alive by struggle, a struggle that must incorporate love, conciliation, freedom, and hope. Freire's message is essential in a world where most people who can influence youth and communities are called upon to spread the news of globalization—that there is only one way to live, one way to do things, one manner of being a human being, and that the only way, form, and manner of educating is subjugated to the interests of the market economy. Freire is a leader in demystifying this pessimistic and fatalistic position. Freire is an inspiration to those who believe that, in spite of all propaganda, we can still become decent human beings and live meaningful lives without necessarily compromising our existence by making it a mere commodity. These principles by themselves justify our need for hearing more, reading more, and enjoying another work by Paulo Freire—one of the last pieces produced during his prodigious journey among us—with plenty of love, wisdom, and solidarity.

Chapter 2

Pedagogy of Solidarity

Paulo Freire

I always, in circumstances like this, ask myself, what will I speak about? What could I say to you that could help you in your curiosity about education? I will try to make more or less the same speech I made some days ago in one of my recent presentations in the United States. I will try to think of education as if I were alone in my studio at home. When I do that I ask myself some questions. One of the questions, for example, and usually the first one we can ask ourselves about education is precisely, what is education or, in other words, what is it that education can be and what are the foundations of the existence of educational practice, as we understand it, as we, human beings, do it. After that, we may have other questions to ask and perhaps some answers to give.

In asking about some fundamental reasons for the existence of education we are asking about our very existence in the world. I believe that it is impossible to understand education without a certain comprehension of human beings. There is no education without the presence of human beings. And what do we have as human beings—women and men—which creates in ourselves the need and the possibility of doing education? How do we create the possibility to educate and to be educated? At this point we are grasping something that we may call the

Pedagogy of Solidarity, Paulo Freire, Ana Maria Araújo Freire, and Walter de Oliveira. © 2014 by Ana Maria Araújo Freire and Walter Ferreira de Oliveira, pp. 15–34.

nature of human beings. The nature, not understood as something that simply exists, and not something that exists independently of history, a priori of history, but, on the contrary, as a creation within history. That is, as historical beings we are engaged in the constant process of creating and re-creating our own nature. Because of that we really are not, we are becoming. That is, in order for us as human beings to be, we need to become. We need not to be—if we just are, we stop being. We are precisely because we are becoming.

This process of being and not being, the process of becoming, explains our presence in history and in the world. It also explains that as human beings, historical beings, we are uncompleted beings. We are unfinished beings. But the trees are also uncompleted beings and the lions are also uncompleted beings, but they do not know that. Even if they know, they cannot discover; they are not conscious of their knowledge, as we are.

If we are uncompleted beings—the trees, the lions, and us—, why, then, speak about education and why, then, talk about us? Why can't we talk about education and discuss the behavior of trees? The trees and the lions also communicate among themselves. We have at home a couple of German shepherds and they have a good relationship with kids. They do not educate the kids, but they do some things that, at their level, work as if they were educators, but they are not really educators.

I am sure that from a metaphysical point of view what explains the reason for the existence of education is fundamentally the fact of being an uncompleted being and having the consciousness of this uncompletedness. Education finds itself at this level. Because of that, we speak about education among us, we speak about the training of animals, we speak about cultivation of trees. But only women and men experience education and the reason for that is that being uncompleted beings and knowing that we are uncompleted beings make education an absolutely indispensable venture. However, when I say education I do not necessarily mean education as we do it today. The education developed by the Greeks belongs to their history, to their moment. In the history of education we have changed, from time to time, the conceptualization of how we deal with children, how we deal with students. Our understanding of childhood is historically mutable. All of these mutations have happened under the influence of the historical and social changes which we have witnessed along history.

The fact is that education is absolutely necessary according to the very nature of human beings as uncompleted beings who are conscious of that; but, precisely because human beings are historical beings, education is also a historical event. This means that education changes in time and space.

For example, it is a mistake—and when I say a mistake I am being polite—for a nation, a state, to think that it can educate other societies and other peoples. It is as if, for example, Brazil, impregnated with power (and fortunately this does not exist), decided to educate the world through Paulo Freire. Then Brazil would send Freire to Asia, Africa, North America, to teach other peoples to be like Brazilians. This would be absurd, this is absurd, and the name for this is imperialism. Besides this political dimension, we have also, a philosophical mistake in this, a cultural mistake, a misunderstanding of what is the meaning of culture. I am a Brazilian, I am my language, I am my food, I am my weather, as you are your language, your weather, your food, your feelings, your dreams. And we cannot export dreams.

Once, at the beginning of my travels around the world, I was asked, I don't remember where, "Paulo, what can we do in order to follow you?" And I said, if you follow me, you destroy me. The best way for you to understand me is to reinvent me and not to try to become adapted to me. Experience cannot be exported, it can only be reinvented. This is the historical nature of education. This is why, for example, the main responsibilities for educators are for changes in education. The persons responsible for education should be entirely wet by the cultural waters of the moment, of the space.

This is why, also, I am sure that a foreigner, an American professor, or a Chilean, or French, or Indian, can go to Brazil to help us to change education in Brazil. But he or she can only do that if, firstly, he or she really knows something about Brazil; secondly, if he or she is eager to learn about Brazilian reality; and thirdly, if he or she is humble enough to re-think himself or herself. Without these conditions, it is better for all of us that this person stays at home, do not go there to try to educate us. The same rules apply to me. I am sure that I also can give a contribution to educators in this country, but I have, first of all, to respect them, respect their knowledge about their country, their culture, and their history. And then I can say "What do you think of that?" And I have to be open to learn about the local reality. Out of that, what we have is authoritarianism and disrespect for the other. And this is another aspect that makes me believe that education is developed in history, is born in history, and changes historically as we are built historically and not only genetically. Finally, we are the relationships between genetic heritage and cultural and historical heritage. We are these relationships.

After recognizing that education is a consequence of our uncompletedness, about which we are conscious, we can then try an exercise of critical reflection. We can think of an educational situation in order to try to grasp its constitutive elements. Let us do this exercise. Let us think of an educational situation, no matter if this situation happens at home, informally, between parents and kids, or formally at school, and it does not matter if the school is a primary school or a university.

First of all, when we think of this educational situation, we may think that every educational situation implies it is, historically, in the presence of the educator, the professor, the teacher, on the one hand, and the educatee, the student, the learner, on the other hand. They each have their specificity. And, I would like to say, because sometimes people misunderstand me and say that for me there is no difference between teacher and student, between the professor, the educator, and the learner. I never wrote that, I never said that; but, because I insist on criticizing the arrogance of teachers, because I insist on criticizing the authoritarianism of professors, some people conclude that for me teachers and students are the same and that I do not recognize any kind of authority. No, I never said that because I think that this is a mistake, this is wrong. Teachers are teachers and students are students. If the students were like the teachers, we would not need to say teachers and students because all of them would be the same. We could say just teachers or just students, because they would be all alike. Secondly, we could not understand the very process in which they are immersed. Then, it is necessary to underline the differences, the specificities of both, and their tasks, the tasks that must be accomplished by both.

When we think about any educational situation, we may discover that in every educational situation, besides the two sides, the two poles—students and teachers—there is a mediating component, an object of knowledge, to be taught by the teachers and learned by the students. This relationship is, for me, more beautiful when the teacher tries to teach the object, which we may call the contents of a program, in a democratic way. In this case, the teacher makes a sincere effort to teach an object that he or she supposedly already knows, and the students make a sincere effort to learn the object that they do not know yet. However, the fact that the teacher supposedly knows and the student supposedly does not know, does not prevent the teacher from learning during the process of teaching, and the student from teaching, in the process of learning. The beauty of the process is exactly this possibility

of re-learning, of exchanging. This is the essence of democratic education.

Even now, while I am repeating, to a certain extent, and revisiting,
and re-speaking about some knowledge that I have for lots of years, I
am refreshing this knowledge. It is as if I were proving, testing, and renewing the knowledge I already have. Maybe I am knowing better what I
already knew. Of course, if we decided to stay with this question, on the
relationships between students and teachers and their roles, we could
spend hours of thinking, of reflection. We could, for example, extend
the question to examine our experience as practical teachers. For example, what am I doing as a teacher in biology, or in history, or mathematics? What am I teaching? What does teaching mean to me? And, in
examining these questions, I would have to ask: Am I being consistent
in my practice with the way I think of teaching? I can think democratically about teaching, but in my teaching practice I may be authoritarian,
which happens a lot. It is not uncommon that our speech has nothing
to do with our practices. This is very common among politicians, for example. One thing is the political candidate's discourse, another thing is
the elected politician's practice. After being elected, the politicians have
nothing to do with the candidates' speeches. And, my struggle includes
an effort for all of us educators to grasp, to live, this coherence between
what we do and what we say.

The first and the second conditions of education are, thus, the presence of teachers and students and the mediation of their relationships
by the objects of knowledge, which we call the contents of education.
Another characteristic of the educational experience, as important as
the existence and relationships between teachers and students, is the
quality of the process of education, which has important implications
from the technical, philosophical, structural, and political viewpoints.
In analyzing qualitatively the process of education I would like to high-

light the quality of directivity, starting from the proposal that there is no education that is not directive. Directivity of education does not necessarily mean authoritarianism. Directiveness in education, philosophically and epistemologically understood, means that education, as a process, means something that goes beyond itself. Let me try to clarify.

When one teaches, one's moral responsibility is to realize that one cannot teach what one does not know. I have to know first, in order to teach second. But in order to teach, one needs more than knowing. Let us suppose that I teach syntax in the Portuguese language, which I taught when I was very young. I have to know syntax and Portuguese, but I must also know in favor of what, in favor of whom, in favor of what dream I am teaching syntax and Portuguese. As a consequence of thinking in favor of whom, in favor of what, in favor of what dream I am teaching, I will have to think against whom, against what, against what dream I am teaching. From my point of view it is impossible to be a teacher without asking these questions. If we consider education in its philosophical, epistemological, and historical dimensions, we cannot escape from these questions. I call this quality of education of going beyond itself—the fact that the process of education always goes beyond itself—directivity of education. Beyond means that education is always related to a dream, and the teachers must have their own dreams, their own utopia.

I feel very sad when a teacher says to me, "I teach mathematics, my dream is mathematics." No, the dream cannot be just mathematics. I teach mathematics because I believe it is necessary for a society to have less discrimination. The main dream, the fundamental dream, is not mathematics. Mathematics is very important, but it has to be at the service of something. I want mathematics to work in favor of me, a human being.

Another thing that has also to do with the directiveness of education is when the teacher, in his or her relationships with the students, exaggerates his or her authority. And it becomes kind of honorable, in the view of some teachers, to castrate the students' freedom. The opposite occurs when the teacher's authority disappears and the freedom of the students becomes exaggerated. In this case there is no freedom, but license. I reject both of these possibilities—on the one hand the authoritarianism and the license of the teacher and on the other hand the authoritarianism of the students.

An important question, then, from which we cannot escape is the contradiction between authority and freedom. I want to say to you, and maybe this has already been understood from the readings of my papers, that I love freedom. I love freedom and I try to understand it in such a way that recently, in my last book, I wrote that authority is an invention of freedom. Freedom invented authority in order for freedom to continue to exist. Because without limits freedom cannot succeed, freedom loses itself. However, a big mistake is that in creating authority, freedom risks losing freedom. But this is one of the most beautiful things in the human experience, the risk of dying, the risk of disappearing. One important characteristic of human beings is the possibility of risking and one of the most beautiful things is to run the risks.

The trees also have risks, but don't run the risks. The trees are here today but tomorrow an administrator may decide to cut down the trees and the trees have no way of acknowledging it. We risk dying but we run that risk. We assume the possibility of risking. Without risks there would be no possibilities for human existence. It would be something very bland, very insipid. Human existence would be like water with no salt.

I have proposed that it is very important to recognize this quality of education, this possibility of going beyond itself, which implies the right and the duty of teachers and also of students to have dreams and to struggle for their dreams. Of course we have to also be aware of the rights the teachers don't have, of imposing upon the students their dreams. Teachers should not have to hide their dreams, but they have the duty to say that there are different dreams. Consider, for that matter, the university. The university that has only progressive teachers is a disaster. The university that has only reactionary teachers is another kind of disaster. What youths need is precisely the testimony of the difference and the right to discuss the difference. This is what should happen. How beautiful it is for the students who finished listening to a progressive teacher speaking about utopia, criticizing, for example, a neoliberal discourse, which is spreading now the terrible ideology of fatalism around the world, [and then] to listen, after that teacher leaves, to another teacher defending the neoliberal thought. Someone may ask, "Paulo, don't you think that this is very confusing, that we can confuse the students?" And I say, it is fantastic that we confuse the students. They have to learn how to deal with confusion; they have to be formed in such a way as to not accept everything that the teachers say, to criticize the teachers. This is not a lack of respect, and in this aspect I am very conservative, I demand respect as a person and as an educator. You have every right to reject my knowledge and wisdom, to criticize my thinking; but, you have an obligation to respect me and I do not accept being disrespected. And, it is possible to be absolutely serious and democratic and at the same time to demand respect. From my perspective, the more the university stimulates different ways of thinking, of dreaming, the more the students will have the possibility of making choices in the future, and that means the more the youth will have opportunities for producing knowledge.

Let's talk about another quality of educational practice that I am very fond of and that touches me from time to time: the strong kind of respect that the teacher must have for their students and for their colleagues. I think that teachers should avoid the kind of confrontation into which they sometimes fall vis-à-vis students and other teachers. They should avoid badmouthing other teachers in their classes. I believe this is a big mistake. This has to do with another dimension of the process of education, absolutely necessary to education, which is the ethical aspect of educational practice. The teacher has to be more and more ethical. I would never say that the teacher has to be a puritan, but we need to show purity to the students.

We have to give examples. It is absolutely important to know that education demands examples, the testimony. The speech, the democratic speech of the teacher that is not founded in practice, that distorts, that denies practice is a contradiction. For example, when I was living in Genève, a friend of mine who is a psychologist was taking a special seminar about authoritarian societies at the University of Genève. She told me that the teacher was very good, very competent. When he was teaching, my friend used to look at his eyes, she could not take her eyes from his eyes she so admired his teaching. One day she was in class as usual and she wanted to smoke, so she went through her purse to get cigarettes while she continued to look at the teacher's eyes. She took a cigarette and lighted it, while still paying attention to what the teacher was saying. The teacher stopped and asked her, "Lady, do you know who I am?" And she said, "Of course, you are the teacher," and he said, "Then I don't understand how is it possible that you try to smoke here without my permission." And my friend took her things and said, "I am finished with my experience with you and I take it as a very good example of authoritarianism. Thank you very much, and good bye."

I interpret the story in the following way: one thing would be for the teacher to say to the students, "Let's discuss smoking. I would thank you if it is possible for you not to smoke." In this case the teacher is expressing his position but he is giving the students an opportunity to discuss, to argue, if it would be allowed. A different situation would be if there was an administrative rule, if the administration had established that one could not smoke in the classroom. Still another thing was what the teacher did, forcing students to do something without the students having the opportunity of discussing it. I believe the story underlines an ethical dilemma.

There is no education without ethics; and, precisely because ethics walks constantly very close to aesthetics, because there is a certain intimacy between beauty and purity, education is also an aesthetic event. I am so radical in my understanding of education as an art that I even do not accept the much used expression, "education through art." When I say that I do not accept it, it is not because I think it is wrong to say that but because I believe it is redundant, because education is in itself an experience of beauty. Because education has to do with formation and not with training, education goes beyond the mere transference of techniques. I see as dangerous the possibility of education collapsing into technique, of being transformed into mere technique, into a practice that loses sight of the question of dreaming, the question of beauty, the question of being, the question of ethics. That would be an education just for production, just for marketing.

Education cannot be just technique because education has as a characteristic, another quality, that I call politicity. The politicity of education is the quality that education has of being political. And one principle related to this quality is that education never was and never will be neutral. I am not talking here about parties, about the Democrats or the Republicans, but about analyzing the nature of the educational process. Of course the political parties have not only the right but the duty of building a conception of education. How is it possible to be a politician without becoming a teacher, without becoming an educator? The political parties in their struggle have to show to the people what they understand as education, what it means to prioritize in education, what they believe the budget of education must be, and so on. But, independent of the platforms of the political parties, education is a political event.

However, and besides the qualities I have spoken about thus far, the process of education also implies technique, also implies the utilization of technological instruments. It is impossible today for an industrialized country to develop education without using sophisticated elements of technology. When I was secretary of education for the city of São Paulo, I introduced computers in the public schools. We invited as a consultant a great disciple of an eminent professor of the Massachusetts Institute of Technology (MIT), Seymour Pappert, and we gave access to computers to the kids in the slums of São Paulo. The question for me is not to avoid the use of technology but to understand and to properly develop a policy for the use of technology. The question is not to be against technology, but to become very clear on what are the politics that inform the use of technology. In other words, we are using technology in favor of whom and in favor of what, and against whom and against what.

Technology is an instrument, a cultural and historical instrument. As such, the introduction of technology has to be considered in its historical and cultural dimensions. We cannot impose upon a culture the use of technological instruments that are three, four hundred years beyond the people's reality, beyond the people's feelings. This is why being an educator or an administrator in education implies that one has constantly to increase, to improve, their understanding of other cultures, in order to have a more and more fresh mind. And when I say another culture, I don't mean necessarily another country. We may have different cultures in the same country, sometimes within the same state, within the same city. That is why the educator must be aware of the culture, of the history, of the feelings; he or she has almost to guess the feelings of the students, of the people.

Finally, if we understand, from these different perspectives, the raison d'être for education and the process of education, and we make a point to be consistent, we, as educators and teachers, have to make choices, In making choices we have to be consistent with our choices in order to avoid unacceptable contradictions with our practice. If my choice is to be a democratic educator my speech has to be in tune with that choice, has to be consistent with my practice in such a way that at some point my speech is already my practice. If we do not behave in that way we can not only lose ourselves, but we also can make students lose themselves.

Thank you very much.

Questions and Remarks from the Audience

Q: Dr. Freire, I am interested in knowing about the relationships between constructivism and what you have been teaching and writing about for so many years. There is a lot of research and practice nowadays that advocates for a more constructivist approach to education. In regard to the students who have acquired more responsibility for their own learning in such a way that teachers have become mediators of that learning, at what point in history did constructivism borrow from your ideas and how similar are those ideas?

PF: In answering your question I may have to ask the people here to forgive me for a possible lack of humility on my part. I am sure, and this I consider as a lack of humility, that I have everything to do with constructivism and that constructivism has everything to do with me. From my point of view, it is impossible to think today of constructivism without mentioning, of course, Piaget and Vygotsky. I am not comparing myself to these two extraordinary men, but I would say that I have treated and discussed, in these last thirty-five years, some of the fundamental statements and principles of constructivism. Sometimes people ask me the same question in Brazil and I always feel inhibited because

I have to say the truth. Also, sometimes they ask me another question, which is why do you never use the word constructivism? And my answer is, because I never felt the need for it. I discuss the reality of education as I see it, as I do it. And I thank you very much again for the question, because it allows me to lose a little bit of humility and this is good from time to time.

Q: Do you have any explanation as to why so many educators still believe in an education that is neutral and value-free?

PF: This is very hard to explain but I am sure that one of the reasons for that, even though these educators don't know it, is the power of ideology. Interestingly enough, people deny nowadays the very existence of ideology. There is no more ideology, no more history, no more social classes, no more dreams, no more utopia, no more hope, and so on. In my point of view, the only way to deal with ideology is through ideology. Only ideologically can I say that ideology disappeared. The discourse that denies the existence of ideology is, in itself, tremendously ideological. But ideology continues to be very powerful. We interject ideology, we incorporate it, we put it inside of us. I have an example of that kind of interjection that happened to me.

After *Pedagogy of the Oppressed* was published in the United States in 1971, I received a lot of letters, mainly from American women, asking me why I used language in that book that denied the presence of women in the world. I was asked about my language in the *Pedagogy of the Oppressed* that many American women said in their letters was helpful to them but was nevertheless contradictory. The book says, for example, that only men can save the world. Why not women too, the women would ask me. This is a good example of the power of ideology. I was born in 1921. In 1971, I was fifty years old. At that age I was still saying what I was taught to say, which means what I was taught to understand, what I was taught to believe. I was taught through the use of syntax, which for many is a neutral element. I learned in my educational experience that when we say men we include women, and that is a lie. If I say here, "all the women in the world," all the men are not included. So how is it possible to say that if I say all the men in the world the women are included? They are not. However, it took me a long time to understand that, and I owe that understanding to American women. I tell this story in *Pedagogy of Hope*, which is a revisiting of *Pedagogy of the Oppressed*, and I regard this as an example of the power of ideology. It is precisely the power of ideology that still makes some teachers believe that syntax is neutral, that education is neutral.

Another aspect of ideology is the question of interest and fear. Let's consider, for example, the interest that comes from the fear of losing a job, the fear of risking. Many of us at some point in life come to think "It is better to keep my job in peace, I don't have to discuss this question of politicity, of history, this is too dangerous to discuss." But if we really want to analyze the meaning of education, what happens to education, what is happening to our societies, we cannot avoid the political character of our existence, the political character of education, the political character of social life. Yet many times we avoid discussing the political character of education because it is risky; it may even put our job at risk. Fear, in that case, keeps us silent about these and also about many other issues.

So, to answer your question, in my point of view, to the extent that women and men became able through the millenniums of history to create the human world, which is different from the animal world, and to the extent that we created history and time, that is, human time, we can no longer analyze human existence without considering our political nature. And, this happens in spite of the fact that the political parties as they are now may disappear, because they are becoming more and more incapable of answering some crucial questions raised in our post-modern reality. In essence, what I want to say is that human existence is a political experience, and education, as an important dimension of human existence, constitutes a political experience, just as the Greeks considered it.

Q: *If education is a process of becoming, don't we run the risk of stagnation when we conclude that we learned something?*

PF: This is a very interesting question both from a philosophical and from an epistemological point of view. To answer that question we need to talk about the historicity of knowledge. To the extent that human knowledge can be developed as a part of history, inside of history, the knowledge we produce can never be considered as the ultimate one. What we consider as knowledge today may not be considered as knowledge tomorrow and maybe was not considered as knowledge yesterday. The possibility of becoming, which is a characteristic of human beings, is also characteristic of our production of knowledge. Then, when we acquire knowledge, we are not necessarily completing ourselves, we are only inserting ourselves in the permanent process of re-creating, of re-knowing.

Q: *You wrote a text on the question of extension and communication in the rural environment, where you talked about the idea of transferring knowledge from the top down. You also wrote, in the same style, about the banking model of education, where knowledge works as a bank deposit and not as an egalitarian power relationship. Tonight it seems to me that the banking method was used here, your knowledge being deposited upon us in the audience. You were using the banking method as an extension. Do you think that extension is an adequate approach in a context like this but not in others? What, then, is adequate?*

PF: I find it very easy to answer you. First, I think I was not extending anything tonight. Secondly, I think that I was not making a transfer of knowledge. You may remember that I have constantly talked about the need for students to have a critical view of educators and of education— and I do not want to say that people here are my students, but rather an audience of listeners. The problem of banking education is not only related to the educator but to the fact that knowledge cannot be swallowed, it must be conducted. What we did here tonight was to take advantage of the possibilities of language, a situation in which one person came, talked to others, not presenting his speech as the truth, but as his convictions. At the beginning I stated that I would not provide the answers but my answers to some questions. So you have the right to give your answers, to think about education and to tell me, for example, that from your point of view education is not a way to promote the completeness of beings, that education is like a gift from God. And I have the right to say "No, God has nothing to do with this." God does not come to the world to teach us anything. He or she has already taught us. We human beings have to create history, science, technology, and the politics of education.

I did not come here to transfer knowledge but to challenge you. For example, have you not felt tired in trying to follow the movement of my thoughts? I think you may have. If you have not felt tired it is because you have not followed, because one thing I try to do every time I teach, every time I speak, is to challenge people, to try to bring them inside the intimacy of my thoughts. They must feel tired as much as I feel tired, and that is not because I am speaking English, which is not my first language. Of course, I have much more liberty in Portuguese, more possibilities of expressing myself. But I also feel tired because when I speak, I think. And I do not think only about what I have to say but also about what I am talking about because I establish a contradictory relation-

31

ship between my discourse and my thoughts. For me, this process and the relationship established in this way are different from the banking method of education, which I criticize so much. You may consider that I made a banking speech, but I suggest that you go back to my texts and think about tonight's experience and maybe you will see that this is not really a banking-type experience. This is an experience of communication. Of course, banking education, just as I do, also communicates. But my posture, my position vis-à-vis the people who are here listening to me, is characterized by a great deal of respect for all of you.

Q: *When you talked about dreams you mentioned the possibility of the existence of many youth who may not have dreams anymore, who have not been encouraged to dream. When I think about this, it comes to my mind that many adults can also think that things are already decided, already formatted, think about existence as a finished package. What can educators do when dreams are being thus suffocated?*

PF: This possible lack of perspective when we human beings have apparently lost all reasons to have dreams, is not only a dramatic experience, it is a tragic one. This is one of my biggest fears, that humanity falls into this kind of post-modern fatalism. For example, I may talk with a very good economist and he may say to me: "Paulo, from the point of view of economics reality is this way. The globalization of the economy, the emphasis on technology, act in such a way that we have to create unemployment." We have today millions of people without a job. On the other hand, we witness the birth of another kind of analysis, talking about a world without jobs, a world only with leisure. But how is it possible to talk about a world of leisure in Brazil, for example, when we consider that for one to have leisure one has to have first a job. Then I say to my friends in Brazil: "This is absurd, it is immoral, that we finish the twentieth century with seven million people in a state of misery."

And, some post-modern intellectuals keep telling me: "But Paulo, what can we do, this is the reality, the reality is an absence of dreams."

But I will die struggling against this. If all scientists in the world try to prove to me that this is the reality, I will be the last man in the world claiming that this is not the only possible reality! There can be another reality. Reality does not necessarily need to be like this one, because of the reasoning of a few, because of the interests of a few powers. Reality can be transformed and must be transformed. The fact is that my dreams remain alive; the power of my dreams leads me to say to you one more time, "Please do not give up." Do not allow this new ideology of fatalism to kill your need to dream. Without dreams there is no life, without dreams there is no human existence, without dreams there are no human beings.

A Dialogue

Pedagogy of Solidarity

The idea behind this seminar, which took place on March 25, 1996, was to take advantage of the presence of Professor Paulo Freire and explore a few themes that had been proposed by an interdisciplinary group of scholars from the United States, Canada, and England. The group had collaborated for a few months before Paulo's arrival, and using a dialogical method had stimulated each other to participate in examining and clarifying the themes.

Walter Oliveira (WO): Today we hope to provide a few answers to the questions we've been working on as a group for the last few months. We have three basic themes and we understand that the dialogue may not be exclusively tied up into these themes, because we understand that the dialogical approach may lead us into different directions. The themes have been developed into three discussion topics:

   I.   The educated person in educational communities.

  II.   Youth and the future.

 III.   Spirituality and vocation.

Pedagogy of Solidarity, Paulo Freire, Ana
Maria Araújo Freire, and Walter de Oliveira.
© 2014 by Ana Maria Araújo Freire and
Walter Ferreira de Oliveira, pp. 35–64.

Paulo Freire (PF): The questions presented, and some of them have already been elaborated by this working group, are a text in itself. I have found it fantastic, a very good proposal for discussion. It would be too optimistic to think that we can have an exhaustive discussion about all of the issues that we have listed. But, while it is not possible to have an exhaustive discussion, it will be useful to try to discuss some ideas related to these issues in a way that will lead us and others into deepening the examination of these and other related questions. It is possible I have never had an experience like this. It is very good.

WO : *It seems to me that to a great extent these themes are interconnected; they are not separated from each other. On the other hand, we can examine each one separately for the sake of a more focused discussion. For each of the three general themes, sets of questions have been formulated by the working group. For the first theme, the first question refers to "quality of education":*

Which quality or qualities do you consider most important for educated persons to possess in the twenty-first century? Part of what we want to address here is how we think about education and how we think and act on the main goals and purposes that education serves.

PF: In being asked this question I have some reactions, some answers. I insist on saying that I will tell you how I see the question, that is, how I react to the question. But I am also convinced that this is not the answer, because I believe in the accepted totality of the answers and in the possibility of different answers.

First of all, it is not easy for me to think about the questions because they relate to a tomorrow not close to me. What I want to say is that I prefer to think of them in terms of today, because the more I think of today, the more I assert myself, the more it is possible to see tomorrow. We can foresee some of the qualities, some of the challenges which we have already. Some of the qualities needed in the last and in the next century have been experienced by us in past centuries. It does not come from the point of view of chronology. It is 1996 but we are already living in the next century.

For example, let us think of the speed with which technology establishes or creates change. Two to three centuries ago the changes happened in the time of one century. We could live a century in more or less in the same way, with not many changes in lifestyle overall. Today, technology changes almost every day and proposes new habits, new answers. In the field of computers and communications, for example, what has been done in the last few years is incredible. With a globalized economy, it is true that technological revolutions or changes are being done in ways that affect deeply the process of education. Because of the speed of technological change, which constantly promotes life changes, I am sure that one of the qualities that we have to be concerned about in education is the quality of getting or creating the ability to answer different challenges with the same speed that things change. This is one of the demands of contemporary education. We need to form and not to train.

There is a very radical difference between training and forming, it is not just a semantic question. Forming is something deeper than just training. Forming is needed precisely to change the great and beautiful critical mind of ours: to increase intuitive curiosity which characterizes us as human beings. Where there is life there is curiosity—among the trees, among the other animals. But in our case curiosity has gone to another level. From the point of view of education, one of the more serious questions regarding the immediate present and the morrow is how to form people in order for them not to get lost in the changes which technology creates.

Question from the Audience (Q): The process of technology, as well as the demands imposed on students by a system that emphasizes training over formation, may seriously interfere in the promotion of such qualities as improved critical abilities. The current system emphasizes, for example, quantity over quality. For example, students may be called to assimilate an enormous amount of information in a certain period of time, against being stimulated to examine very well certain issues, which could help them to develop their critical abilities. By the same token, class discussions, and even discussions in professional meetings, have to be curbed because it seems that there is never time enough to discuss in-depth certain issues. Students have to constantly rush to satisfy the demands presented by educators.

PF: And now I ask, can we think of an education or process of education in which the educators call the students not to read in one semester three hundred books but instead to read very well one book, to the point that the student feels that she or he is able to rewrite the book that was read? Is it possible to educate while forcing the students to read three hundred books in one semester? The result of this kind of educational process is that students live under tension, and that undermines their ability to learn. This tension is so great that some students commit suicide. This phenomenon happens all over the world. Is it because of a practice of education in which students are trained instead of being formed to reach knowledge instead of producing knowledge? How can educators help to create opportunities for the students to answer the challenges presented by technology? In the particular case of Latin America, other questions can be asked of our education. Is it possible for example to expect good results from an education centered on the blackboard?

In my point of view, education has the responsibility of creating critical minds, and this responsibility is manifested in the educator challenging at the same time the student's curiosity and creativity. How can one be a critical mind if one is not able to create and recreate?

In my point of view there is no evolution without a strong desire, a will, to do new things. And I question again: is education all over the world generating an experience of creativity or the conquering experience of repetition? For example, what does it mean to commit mistakes? If we take the perspective of an education that works with the responsibility of challenging curiosity and creativity on an everyday basis, we have to have respect for mistakes. From this educational perspective, a mistake is not a sin but an integral part, an important moment, in the process of knowledge, or, to be more precise, of the process of creation of knowledge. From the perspective of an education that promotes creation of knowledge, I cannot be afraid of committing a mistake because I commit a mistake to the extent that mistakes are consequences of risks and risking is an absolutely necessary part in the process of confronting the challenges of technological society. Therefore, another quality for the educator of the twenty-first century is the vision that risking must be encouraged, and a desirable consequence of risking is committing mistakes. The educator must then be prepared to work with risk and to deal with mistakes in a positive, encouraging, and challenging way.

When I was secretary of education for the city of São Paulo I brought up the topics of risking and mistakes in my discussions with the teachers. I used to ask first grade teachers: "please don't underline in red the grammatical errors of the students because the more you do that the more you inhibit, the more you create fear. Instead of creating fear, talk to the student and explain how to go beyond that; talk to all students about that." The educator must find practical forms of practicing this promotion of creativity, and this is just one example. We must re-create constantly our praxis as educators, challenging students to be aware and not to be sleeping, that is, to have voice instead of receiving the voice of the teachers, to develop their autonomy, to be themselves and not to be the reflex of the teachers.

Q: Do you think that that kind of education is in the best interest of the state, when we think of the state as an apparatus of controlling and reproducing society? I don't think teachers do what they do just because they don't know how to do it better. I think that teachers are compelled to do what they do because it is in the best interest of the state that is controlled by politicians.

PF: Your question is a very good example of how education cannot be neutral. That is, there is a dimension in the matrix of educational practice which I call "politicity." Politicity is nothing but the quality of being political. When I speak about the politicity of education I am not referring to party politics, in the case of the United States to the Republicans or the Democrats. The parties, of course, have the right and the duty to have their conception of education. Political platforms coming from the political parties should reflect their understanding of education. In this country, I don't know whether it is possible because, in my point of view, the parties here are just one. But this is not the case in Brazil. The conception of education is very different for the different parties. But here, when I am speaking about the politicity of education, I am not talking about party politics, in spite of considering the parties' right to their own conceptualizations of education and their right to fight for putting it into practice.

Among other things your question has to do with the government's political decision to work within the perspective of a democratic education. It is a political decision. Once again, when I was secretary of education in São Paulo I fought for a much less elitist education. Brazilian education is deeply elitist. My goal, considering the constraints of time in my term, was not to do away with elitism, because we would not have enough time, but I fought to diminish the elitization of education. That was a political decision. Secondly, I fought for diminishing the utilitarianism of Brazilian education. I fought for improving the democratic experience of education and also fought for forming the teachers. With that in mind I established programs at the University of São Paulo, the University of Campinas, and the Catholic University of São Paulo. They offered us about sixty excellent professors of different branches of philosophy, linguistics, political science, and sexology. We developed programs for formation and worked with 35,000 teachers responsible for children's literacy. Without these kinds of political initiatives, and without investing in formation, not merely training, of educators, it is very difficult to promote an education that promotes critical thinking, one that prepares students and teachers to respond to the challenges posed by life changes. In the Brazilian case there is still another issue of no less importance, the salary of the teachers. It is not possible to expect a teacher earning USD$100 a month to have a good performance, because with USD$100 she or he cannot even buy newspapers to read. It is therefore imperative that we show the educators that we respect them and demonstrate in practice our commitment to help the teachers in their process of permanent formation. To finish examining your question, in many cases governments are not at all interested in issues which are intrinsically political, that is, when these issues reflect what I call the politicity of education. Governments are usually not interested in forming teachers, they are interested in training them. Governments are not interested in developing an education able to stimulate critical minds.

Essentially, the construction of my response to the question is that one of the duties and one of the rights of progressive teachers has been, and will continue to be in the next century, to fight, to struggle, to mobilize, and to organize themselves to fight. If we live in a true democracy, the struggle of the teachers for a better education cannot be stopped, as well as the struggle of the workers, of the doctors, and of other professionals for better work conditions, which lead to a better society. Without such a struggle I have to tell you that I don't believe in good results.

I believe that the struggle to change reality is part of the nature of human beings. To achieve humanization we must struggle to change reality, instead of just adapt ourselves to reality. I always say that I personally did not come to the world in order to adapt myself to the world; I came to change. Maybe I won't change it, but at least I need to know that I could change and that I must try. If I did not change, it might have happened for some reason, but not because God did not want me to. Do you see, then, the original question leads to another question: How is it possible to fight? Okay this is a question for all of the teachers all over the world. This is also a question for the people: How to struggle? I am making reference to political struggle, but I agree with you that your question pushes us to lots of other questions.

Q: I like to think of the concept of struggle as renewal, and I'd like to think that in the United States renewal is a part of our institutions. We have put into effect institutions, and I'm not talking only about government institutions and educational institutions, but even the business community, that can be committed to a sense of renewal. How do you see struggle as contrasted with renewal?

PF: I think that struggle implies renewal, although I am not convinced that every time we struggle we renew. I strongly believe that we, women and men, become able to interfere in the world which we did not make to the extent that we achieve consciousness of ourselves which in turn is acquired through consciousness of the world. In my point of view, it is the consciousness of the externality of me which makes it possible to get my consciousness in the world, in a way that I will work to change it instead of adapting myself to the world. This is the way to renewal. Organizations constantly state that it is necessary to change, but this commitment to change is not always shown in the organization's everyday practice. There is a moment in which change does not happen

42

anymore; in this moment the organization stagnates and may die. It becomes necessary to recognize the moments in which renewing is no longer being done, so those who are involved in the organization can struggle for the necessary changes. In that sense I don't see opposition between struggling and renewing. On the contrary, I see intervening as a way for renewal.

Q: A second topic in the first question that the group has been discussing relates to what we may call a pedagogy of neighborhoods. The essence of the question is: What would a sustained pedagogy of neighborhoods look like? I think we can get a flow from one topic to another without losing the first one on the quality of education. We are talking about how do we go about integrating the question of a pedagogy of neighborhoods and its transformative power starting from the perspective of teaching in schools.

PF: If we keep in mind the first question concerning some qualities of an educated person and the following topic of struggling in order to create, I would add solidarity as another desirable quality. Solidarity goes side by side with a critical mind. I cannot imagine the world getting any better if we really don't adopt the feeling and immediately become a great mass of solidarity, if we don't struggle for solidarity. These questions are on the side of history, they must become wet by historical waters. When we are very far away from the completeness of history, the questions do not work and the answers do not work either.

Sometimes it seems that we speak about solidarity but we really do not want solidarity to be realized. The idea is, from the perspective of certain groups in the left, that first of all we would have to change radically the material structures of society in order to get into the superstructure and only by performing these structural changes we could see the realization of solidarity in the society. In this kind of dream, the mechanistic dream to transform the material condition of reality, it is assumed that after the promotion of these deep structural changes, in the next day we would have a new man and a new woman, and we could have the installation of solidarity in the society. History demonstrates that it is not like this. Solidarity has to be shaped in our bodies, in our behaviors, in our convictions.

In speaking about local power, which in other words is neighborhood power, we need to confront the process of globalization, to see how globalizing implies suppressing freedom and creativity. Globalization is killing the locality. We need to restore and to invent local power again. Restoring and reinventing local power means to create different possibilities that make possible the experience of solidarity.

The idea of educating cities is very interesting and it seems that suddenly a lot of people grasped this idea. At the same time here we are called to discuss the issue of educating neighborhoods. In a certain way that contains the same idea inside of it. The issue has to do with the character of educators, being therefore a moral issue. For example, when you visit a city that was characteristically developed in the last century, what you see is predominantly sculptures, homage to soldiers, generals, mostly riding horses, in positions of command. In this way, the city teaches the younger generations. I do not think that we should demolish those sculptures, destroy those teachings. We have to keep history. But why don't we start using art to give examples of the kinds of solidarity we envision for the city? Why not commission artists, singers, painters (like in Chicago the painters painted murals on the city)? Why not ask these artists to become effective educators as well? This pedagogic work could also be manifested in different dimensions, for example in the theater.

The artists in the streets are telling the people stories about how to survive with solidarity, with a critical mind, because the neighborhood as a concept is an abstraction. We must conquer the abstraction and apply it to human beings in action. In this way we could have, not in the bureaucratic understanding of the world, the neighborhood becoming a school without the schooling, a school without imposing and asking the students to read three hundred books. The books are not enough. Maybe what is wrong is not asking students to read three hundred books, but the way in which it is asked, as if reading was like consuming knowledge.

Q: *I hear you talking about this occurring in the neighborhoods. Do you think it is naive to think that this can happen within the school systems in the United States? Because the public school teachers are dependent on the universities and I am not sure the universities are teaching teachers how to teach critically?*

PF: No, maybe they are not. But look, somebody once asked me how to teach critically if universities don't do that. First of all, I am awfully naive because the relationship between naiveté and good reason is more dialectical than mechanistic. But, then, I know that it is not easy, that it is very difficult, but it is possible. The issue for us is not to lose this struggle but to experiment with different ways of struggling in order to say that it is possible.

I will try to tell you something about the question. Let us suppose for a moment that I am invited to stay here at this university. I can say that because there is not any reason for me to be invited and no way for me to tolerate the cold. Of course, my intention would be not to just give classes but to work here in favor of solidarity, of change. My first step should be to work in something that I call the ideological map of the institution in which I am now. What do I mean by working on, or creating, or making the ideological map? It means that I need to know who I can count on, with whom I am alike, and against whom I may have to be. If I don't know the levels of power of those opposite me I cannot fight. It is suicide. That is, I have to be militaristic without being or without wanting it. Let us suppose that after researching that I find there are three professors and five students in the department I am in with whom I can have conversations about dreams, and then I begin to work with them about the dreams. At a certain point it would be possible to go beyond the level that we are now at with these eight people. Possibly we could discover one month later another couple of people and one day maybe it is possible for us to make it to eighty people thinking together and maybe we can then start something. This kind of work constitutes a virtue which I call patience in the impatience, that is, I never accept being only patient and never only impatient. In order to work productively in the world one has to be either patiently impatient or impatiently patient. If you are only impatient you destroy your dream before it should be destroyed. But, if you are only patient, the other people destroy your work. You have to be patiently impatient to do things, and if thousands of people would do that, this could transform society.

Changing is difficult but it is possible. If at any moment I would start to believe that changing is impossible, there would be no reason for me to continue to work, there would be no hope. If change is not possible and there is no hope, the only thing that remains is cynicism. If we fall into cynicism, into fatalism, we die even though we are alive.

Q: Getting back to the question of forming and training, I work with college students and younger children. I ask them: "What are the most important forming experiences that you have had in your whole life?" They usually tell me four or five, but they almost always talk about experiences which did not happen in schools. And many of the things they talk about are failures, what we call failures, big mistakes in their lives, maybe things that happened that weren't supposed to have happened but made them who they are. The things that make people who they are mostly don't happen in schools. And those of us who are interested in this neighborhood pedagogy are trying to build on that and learn from that and we believe that the neighborhood is at the center, much like the sun is at the center of our solar system.

PF: I agree. I think that at some moment in history the schools began to become necessary. In a certain moment it may have happened that the schools started to obstruct the normal process of development of persons. In my point of view the question for us today is not to abolish the schools. I never agreed with Ivan Illich, a great friend of mine. For me, what we have to do is not close the schools but make them better, that is, to reorient categorically, politically, the schools. This is one of the tasks the neighborhood can choose. That is, the neighborhood could try to exercise the role of educating the schools inside of it. They could assume the responsibility of forming and reforming the schools which are in their geography. But, for the neighborhood to do that, it is first of all necessary to get the real meaning of solidarity, of being solidary.

Individualism is the antithesis of solidarity. Under the individualistic perspective each one thinks of his or her own personal interests and the tendency is for us to close ourselves in ourselves. But I agree with you in this aspect that the neighborhood should have to change the premises and not the schools, change the school but not abolish the schools.

Q: What kinds of experiences formed you in your childhood? How did you become a critical thinker?

PF: This question is very good and very important, philosophically speaking, because until now I have emphasized the need for formation, but in my speeches, even though this is not my way of understanding formation, it was nevertheless as if we would have no responsibility in the process of our own formation. Your question puts this question on the table. We can and we are responsible and we can have a strong role in the process of our own development through assuming our identity and even struggling against the external elements that would prevent us from being who we are. Because of that, I am sure that in the process of forming, in a democratic way we should emphasize to the students from the beginning the duty and not only the right they have to be themselves. This is the question of the autonomy of being, it is absolutely important.

You asked me about my own formation. Today I was telling Walter during breakfast that my father died when he was fifty-two years old and I was thirteen. It is for me very strange today that I am seventy-five years old and older than my father at his death. He died in 1934 and I feel his presence almost as if he were here now. Such was his influence and his presence in my childhood. In our short experience my father gave me a lot. He gave me a serious testimony of respect for others. For example, he experienced very well his opportunity as father but he never went beyond a certain level, he always respected our freedom. He helped us to be free, to accept the necessary limits without which freedom gets lost. With him I learned tolerance. For example, he was a Spiritualist, a follower of Allan Kardec, the French philosopher who created, organized and systematized a spiritualistic doctrine. My mother was Catholic. Of course he was not a churchgoer, he did not believe in the bureaucracy of the church. He did not accept the ways of believing in God offered by the Catholic Church. This was in the first part of the century, constituting a fantastic example of his openness and his courage. I remember when I was seven years old there was a one-week mission in the parish we lived in, which I participated in and I was trained for my first communion in the church. I went to him not to ask his permission but to tell him that on the following Sunday I would go to the church to have my first meeting with God. And he said to me "I will go with you." You cannot realize how that speech marked me until now. That was a deep understanding of tolerance, of respect for the different. Here was a father in a very particular society, a very conservative one. He could say, "No it is a lie, I cannot leave you free to commit a lie, to participate in such a lie." On the contrary, he went to the church and gave me a fantastic example of the absolute and fundamental importance of solidarity, of how respect for the other is absolutely indispensable, how to discuss changes and how to discuss transformation with respect. In comparison, my mother was not as strong as him; but her example is a strongly loving one. I don't know how to make the distinction between the two testimonies, but they were fundamental for my life. They are more important than the testimony of the schools, even the testimony of the neighborhood.

After those first years I kept working on this idea of respect for the different, and I think this was crucial in forming a critical mind. Since I was very young I learned that I also should act, should do things. I was a student who could not just cross life; I had to create life through my own experience of life. In creating these experiences I had good testimonies of good people and also bad testimony, and these testimonies contributed more or less to my formation.

Many of these things cannot be taught but we can challenge students in order for them to grasp the meaning of these things.

Q: *Is there oppression when there is hope?*

PF: This is a crucial question. I am absolutely convinced of the importance of hope but maybe I have to say something about how I understand hope.

First of all, I never saw with good eyes any kind of philosophy or proposal or historical understanding of our presence in the world that does not take into consideration the essence of human beings, the nature of human beings. Of course there are different ways of conceiving the nature of human beings. I go along with the ones that understand the nature of human beings as being shaped, being constituted, in history. This may be one of the reasons why many Christians do not accept that I am also a Christian, because I agree with Marx in some aspects, for example, when he says that it is not possible to deal with our lives prior to history, nothing exists before history. My understanding of human nature starts with history and not before history. I think that we did not or do not have an abstract definition of the nature of history, that we created it here, that we are creating history every day. And precisely because the nature of human beings is historical and has historicity it means that it is not immobilized, that nature changes. This is one of the principles that orient my understanding of education for change. Because if I start from an orientation in history grounded on metaphysics, I start by accepting the principle that our nature has been shaped historically. If our nature has been shaped historically, it is possible to change it historically.

Secondly, I defend the idea that in some moment of our historical journey in the world as unfinished beings we acquire the ability to recognize ourselves as unfinished beings. Trees are also unfinished beings, lions are also unfinished beings, but maybe they don't know. We human beings know that we are unfinished beings. And precisely because we know, because we have the consciousness of being uncompleted beings, it becomes a contradiction to recognize our incompleteness without engaging in a permanent process of searching for our completeness. It does not mean that being inserted into the process of searching means that we will find the things we are looking for. One of the beauties in the struggle of life, of existence, is precisely the possibility of getting or not getting. Even in those situations when we know what we are trying to get, it does not mean that we will get it. It means that the holistic understanding of history, the understanding of history as a whole process including the things we are looking for, is not a mechanistic understanding. In this perspective instead of just thinking about a future, we must problematize it.

I think of the future as a possibility. Then for me the future is not something that will have to be like it's been said it will be. To accept that the future is a possibility, implies that there are different possibilities for the future and that we have to realize that we have to mobilize ourselves to organize ourselves in order to dream. We have dreams about the future. The conceptualization of future as a possibility brings the idea that the future is not something beyond our ability to influence, some entity waiting for us to arrive. On the contrary, according to this profile of its being a possibility, the future is nothing but transformation—the transformation of today.

The question now is, how could I assert myself in this permanent process of searching without hope? Then hope is not just a crazy idea, a foolish dream of the people: hope has its foundation.

The business of questioning is always fascinating, and as questions always lead to other questions, then the question of responsibility comes up. I came to the world not to adapt myself, but to assume the responsibility for being here; being here means to interfere in this here today. And without hope, how could I do that? If we follow this line of thought we may be led to understand, for example, why the ideology of oppression always injects a certain fatalism in the oppressed. This fatalism is instilled by having the oppressed believe that no solution for them can become a reality, that reality is unchangeable. By the same token, the more the oppressor discovers that reality is not unchangeable, the less the oppressor sleeps well. As a consequence, one of the things to do for the oppressed people is to work on the question of hope, to increase hope, hope in spite of it all. Because without hope, there can be no struggle.

I also could say to you that for me there is hope because God does not lie. But this question satisfies only those who believe in God. I respect all those who do not believe in God so I have to try to give them an answer that they might accept. From my perspective, one of the reasons I have hope is because I believe in God. I am convinced that I am more than my body.

A great friend of mine who did not believe in God died recently. A little before he died he said to me, "Paulo, how is it possible for you to believe in that? We are no more than a cadaver." And I said, look, when we die we have a very interesting experience, perhaps more interesting to you because you don't believe in anything else but your body. Then when you die you will have a great surprise because you will discover that you were and you are more than the body. I will not have this surprise because I am already convinced about that. He died, and maybe he is smiling today.

But coming back to exploring the possibility of an answer to the question of the relationship between oppression and hope, I still feel strongly that the situation of oppression works against hope. I believe that the situation of oppression has everything to prevent the oppressed from having hope. Then for the oppressed there is a moment in which hope begins to come back or to be restored. This happens when the oppressed are engaged at some level in a process of struggle. When I say struggle here I mean political struggle and not necessarily a physical fight. There are lots of physical fights which do not bring any kind of hope.

I remember a discussion that occurred some thirty years ago in one of the circles of culture of a literacy program. We were discussing some aspects of "injecting" hope, of how to help in the process of bringing hope to the people. This discussion touched on the very conceptualization of culture. We were realizing that to grasp the meaning of culture is to understand culture as the result of the differences between human beings, and that these differences occur within the context of the natural world which we did not create. We discovered that to transform reality is to create and solidify a culture, that to make a well is as cultural as writing a poem. When we, men and women, discover that by "making" we are creating and re-creating reality, we are grasping the meaning of culture.

I remember that in one of those evening discussions a man said, "Right now I know that maybe Brazil will not even change but I am now sure that this is not because God does not want it." In that moment that man realized that there were other reasons for not changing which had nothing to do with the supernatural. These other reasons have to do with the structures of society. You see, no establishment allows discussing structures. You can discuss the results, the reflex of the structures, but not the structures. It is a very dangerous terrain to be discussed.

Q: And if you cannot discuss the structures, of course there is no hope because there are no possibilities for the deep structural changes that are needed to help the situation of the oppressed.

PF: It becomes clear then that there is undoubtedly a relationship between hope, lack of hope, presence of hope, oppression, struggle against oppression, perpetuation of the establishment of the social structures and the status quo, solidarity, and adaptation to oppression. The lack of hope necessarily leads to a fatalistic position vis-à-vis the reality.

Q: And all of these— lack of hope, fatalism and consequently the absence of struggle, apathy, and lack of solidarity—are instrumental for the perpetuation of reality as is, meaning, of unjust social structures and of oppression.

PF: Exactly. Historically we have always acknowledged fatalism. However, fatalism was mostly existent among workers, especially peasant workers. Today, fatalism is among university economists, among scholars. When the economists affirm that from the point of view of economy we have nothing to do but adapt to the current reality of what has been called globalization, we have to understand that they are saying that there is no hope out of this perspective.

Q: In other words, that we have to accept reality as is, that we have no way of changing it.

PF: Why does globalization have to imply a total impossibility of changing reality? Is it possible that technology has to have that much power over us even though it was created by us? It becomes a very good question to ask whether tomorrow's robots will be in command over the human beings who created them, submitting us to their power. The answers to these questions cannot be provided by technology. I refuse to accept answers to such questions from technology. They have to come from us, human beings, utilizing the power of our critical minds. We have to provide the answers; we owe these answers to ourselves and to the next generations.

The problem of technology, then, is not technological but political. The enactment and implementation of policies dealing with technology, the policies dealing with the process of globalization, are all political issues. Globalization is essentially a political issue.

Q: And fatalism, following this line of thought, is a political attitude, ideologically controlled.

PF: Of course, this fatalism that we see today, championed by certain economists and certain political groups, telling us that there is only one way to go, works in favor of the process of globalization and in favor of creating a situation in which we see ourselves as powerless, transferring our power, the power of human beings, to technology. This fatalism, therefore, has deep political implications. This fatalism today is inside of the male, neoliberal speech all over the world, homogenized, saying the same thing in different languages, preaching the lack of importance of history, telling us that there are no social classes, no ideology, no struggles between classes, no hope, no dreams, and no utopias, and for me this is an ideological lie. As a human being I protest. Because I continue to believe in our power of transforming reality, in our utopias, cultivated over many years of civilization, and I am not even talking as a politician or as an educator, but primarily as a human being.

Q: It seems that fatalism, associated with the neoliberal drive to a global village governed by the market system, based on competition and social Darwinism, tends to lead to a homogenization of cultures, or even the disappearing of cultural differences, with all its perils, including losing sight of other alternatives to the market ruling. It also relies on people having to accept the fact that nothing can stop it, and all we can do is to serve this destiny, to fulfill this prophecy.

PF: Yes, and I refuse to accept this role which is committed to an ideology that contributes to our de-humanization. Again, I did not come to the world just to adapt myself to an offered reality. I recognize the strength of this reality, the power of this reality. Maybe we never had such a powerful reality before, but even this powerful reality has to be seen as changeable and its transformation depends upon our wishes, upon our dreams.

One of the problems we have today is how the financial capital circulates quickly around the world looking for the more profitable places, the places which pay more. This was one of the reasons behind the breaking down of the economy in Mexico, in Argentina, and it almost happened in Brazil. If you say to some economists that there are lots of people in Brazil dying of hunger in the same moment when the production of food in the world could feed twice the population of the world, they say, yes but this is reality and we cannot change it. I say no, this is this reality but we have to change it. It is interesting to notice that when these same kind of people, of that level, the big capitalists, those in command in the world, become objects and see themselves threatened by a fatalistic situation, then they see the possibility of change. After the economic disasters in Mexico, they began to say that it is absolutely necessary for these commanders of the world to begin to regulate, to establish a discipline for protection of the financial capital that circulates around the world. In this situation was perceived the necessity and the possibility of an immediate reorganization. It was perceived that there is a possibility of stopping the problem, of changing the reality. Nevertheless, when it comes to people dying of hunger, there is no possibility for stopping, there is no possibility of reorganizing because this is perceived as an unchangeable situation—it is the reality and that is that. Is it, or not, the power of ideology, the power of those who are able to dictate to others what it is that can be or cannot be done, the power of interpreting and imposing an understanding of life, of reality, and of our own possibilities in the world?

I would like to finish by saying to you that one of my struggles as an educator today is this one, that is, I fight against this kind of fatalism and cry out, "No! No! I am a man and I cannot accept such a terrible reality." My hope is indispensable for me.

Q: Isn't there also a reactionary potential to hoping in the United States because there is this saying that people can be whatever they want to be? Maybe if you work hard enough you will make it, but at the same time that idea goes with the assumption that there is nothing wrong with the system and it is a matter of you trying very hard and working very hard. So, I see that hope, on the one hand, has its potential but also has the potential to reinforce negative attitudes, including from the point of view of education because you have hope that things are going to be better without understanding that for this to happen you have to assume responsibility. Therefore, it is more than just hope, I think; it is hope linked with reality.

PF: I think I understood your question. For me the problem is that often hope has to be critical because there are ways of being naively hopeful, a kind of sweet hope. Religions usually have a strong responsibility for that kind of naive hope, which is precisely the kind of hope you can find in the attitude of resignation. I do not defend this resignation. On the contrary, I defend serious rebellion. But in order to create something more than rebellion, we have to foster attitudes to create the revolutionary. In this case I am not making any kind of reference to traditional revolution. What I want to say is that sometimes in rebellion you have to have much more than indignation. You have the protest, you have the denunciation, but you still have to have the enunciation. That is, at the same time you are denouncing you have to announce, at least the announcement of what should be the drawing of your dream. This is more than rebelling, but it cannot exist without rebellion.

To preach resignation is a sweet way of lying to the oppressed. For example, thirty or forty years ago it was common for a priest, after eating a good breakfast, to say in the church to the people with hunger to be patient because you will get the kingdom of God. He was proposing resignation and not proposing hope. I am against it.

Q: I have been teaching your work for thirteen years in a community course on Pedagogy of the Oppressed and Critical Consciousness. The students pick up nearly everything. But when I get to cultural circles and the need to decode the emotional themes, sometimes I find difficulties in the discussion with the students. What can you tell me about what I can do to get that message across?

PF: Look, when we begin to discuss reality we face the need to discuss some internal questions as well. At that point the discussion begins to become difficult because sometimes we have to touch on our own emotions and feelings. I never forget my first conversation in the 1970s with Erich Fromm in Mexico. I was explaining to him some of the major points of my work and after five minutes of my talking, he finished the conversation because he already knew it. Then he smiled because I said that if I always spoke to people like him I would not speak. He analyzed my work and said in conclusion "what you are doing is a very special kind of psychological, cultural, political, and ideological psychoanalysis." And he said, "I have spent years waiting for this kind of education." He told me, "that is why you cannot be easily accepted by those who have power, because to propose the oppressed think of themselves as not necessarily victims of the society is to work against those who impose their rules on the society."

For those who have power it is fundamental that education becomes only techniques. The reduction of education into techniques is absolutely indispensable for the continuation of a society like this. But at its best, education is much more than a technique, education is an understanding of the world in order to transform it.

But to stay with your question, first of all I think we have to be sympathetic with the strong reactions of people, especially the resistance to examining their own feelings. Our task is difficult. We don't even have scientific technology to help in confronting certain psychological situations, which the psychotherapists confront as well. Nevertheless, truly educators are social psychotherapists, as Erich Fromm very well pointed out. The answer to the question, for me, is to understand, to respect, to be silent in the moments of pain because sometimes people really suffer during the process of education.

I remember one day in Chile in 1966 when during a discussion a young man looked at the educator coordinating the discussion and said, "Look sir, finally what is your point?" This man was angry because the questions were beginning to touch some of his emotional problems. Then, instead of questioning himself, his reaction, his resistance, led him to question the educator and the process of education.

Then my answer is, first of all we have to respect people's feelings. However, we have to do our best in order to help them to get the courage for confronting themselves, because one of the conditions for us to have hope, and therefore to become engaged in any kind of socially significant struggle, is to deal with our own difficulties and not to be angry with the others. Sometimes people feel at ease dealing with their own difficulties, but sometimes there is an enormous resistance. When this happens, maybe we could tell stories that involve the same kinds of feelings which are at stake in a particular moment. In this way we could trivialize the feelings that we are touching on and the fact that we are causing pain. Perhaps we could make these feelings and this pain more ordinary. Maybe it could be useful to create a certain distance, a separate intimacy between us and the problem, because sometimes a question makes us suffer in such a way that we even do not want to think about the question. What we want is to escape, to sleep, and if the educator insists in asking the question and forces me again to face the situation I can feel offended.

An example of a very touchy problem has to do with the question of discrimination. One of the faces of discrimination is the imposition of white English language on black people. One question is how is it possible to teach English to black children in a particular neighborhood if the teacher is not in solidarity, really in solidarity, with the black child? If the teacher does not have scientific information, if the teacher never read or thought about the ideology pervading issues of language and communication, if the teacher is absolutely convinced that white English defines the standard of quality in the world of good language, how is it possible for this teacher to teach black children? It is absolutely impossible. I am not saying that a white teacher should not teach black kids but should teach them acknowledging the differences in syntax in the English used by white and black people. On the other hand, the teacher has to teach the white syntax, not because the syntax of the black children is inferior, not because black English is ugly. The black kids need to learn the white English in order to fight better the white ideology of discrimination. This is how I see it.

Once again we are touching on the problem of respect and on the problem of respecting the cultural identity of the students. Because of these problems I have my doubts concerning the idea of multicultural-ism and multi-linguistics in this country. Multiculturalism, for me, im-plies respect for all cultures and this respect implies that the primary culture does not impose its values on the other cultures.

Q: Did your understanding of Christ shape your understanding of the import-ance of the word as a basic element of dialogue in your writings?

PF: Once, in Europe, some people asked me about the influence of the great educators, the great philosophers, in my work, in my curiosity, and I remember I spoke first about Christ. I understand Christ as a simple educator. I can think of many examples of his fantastic testimony for my understanding of history and of education. I think that we com-mit a great mistake in trying to understand Christ without considering the dialectics between the different moments of his life. For example, we sometimes quote the moment he gave the other face to those who slapped him but not the violent way in which he reacted to the com-mercialization of the temple, because it shows a face of him that was not sweet.

Q: I want to go back for a minute to the student from Chile, the one who was hurt by not seeing the educator's point, and not look at him as a student but look at him as a teacher. This Chilean student from may have taught us something that helps us understand what a teacher is and what the youth worker is. When I say it in my words I want to make sure that my words mean the same to you as they mean to me in our conversation. It seems that the young man taught us that a teacher exists as a question, that the teacher is an interrogation and the teachers' responsibility is to live as a question, so that living as a question is a way to address the world as well as to address the student. In that case, it seems to me that the fact that the student became nervous is a sign that the teacher was doing his job.

PF: A wonderful interpretation. A good teacher makes the students tired and curious. I very much doubt the teacher who keeps his class well behaved.

Q: If the teacher exists as question, then that question is inherent to the struggle because the question is always about the possibility of distance between now and maybe. That is where courage has to walk.

PF: I agree. No comments. Sometimes I get tired of a question, sometimes we get tired, but in my case I have no possibility of getting tired of you because of the language of your abstract thinking. I think that there is a kind of a contradiction between the act of speaking and the possibility of understanding what is spoken by the others. I am much more able to say what I mean in English than understanding you who are native English speakers. I always need help. It implies that I always get tired.

Q: I understood you to say that hope is necessary but not sufficient to overcome oppression. But earlier on, you described one of the qualities of an educated person as being someone who has a critical mind. Apparently, putting those things together, hope plus a critical mind, gets us closer to dealing with oppression. But now you mentioned the idea of solidarity as we've gone along. So, I am thinking that solidarity is another piece. Are you saying that hope plus a critical mind plus solidarity are three of the elements that you would see necessary to overcome oppression?

PF: I would like to clarify that I meant go beyond oppression, past oppression.

Q: Is there a difference between "overcoming" oppression and "going beyond" oppression?

PF: No.

Q: The solidarity of a working class would be one way of thinking about that. But, today in the U.S., it is very hard to say that we have two groups, only those who have and those who have not. Among the "haves" we have lots of groups and among the "have nots" we have lots of groups. Even as I look around our group this morning there are commonalities, but there is unique-ness too. How do you deal with solidarity given the great amount of diversity we now recognize among us?

PF: There are different opportunities in which you can express your soli-darity. In a very broad understanding of solidarity you can be solidary with a billionaire person who is in need, you can be a samaritan. You do not refuse to give him a glass of water in spite of his badness. It is a form of solidarity, it is a kind of human necessity of human beings. But when I speak about solidarity in the context of our discussion this morning, I am mostly referring to the necessary solidarity which people who have the same dreams or similar political dreams have to have among them-selves in order to struggle against the other side. Of course the other side also has to be solidary and they are. Those who have power are soli-dary among themselves in order to prevent the collapse of the totality of power. They demonstrate every day solidarity among themselves. This is also solidarity.

My dream is for a society less ugly, a society in which we can laugh with no falsity, in which knowing is not a problem of seeing, in which there is no discrimination of language, race, or sex. I am not think-ing about a society of angels because angels do not make politics; I am thinking of a society of human beings. We have to have solidarity among those who have similar dreams. This solidarity implies hope and without solidarity and hope it is impossible to struggle.

For me, one of the things I understand scientifically but I cannot accept politically and philosophically is the lack of solidarity among the so-called minorities in this country. In the United States the minorities are really the majority. If they would discover the power of solidarity, which could make them united, that would make a world of difference. If they were united while preserving their own diversity, they would discover they are not minorities; the only minority is the ruling dominance. One of the rights preserved by the dominant minority is to profile the dominated. For example, the colonizers who arrived here said that the natives did not have history until the colonizers came. Because the natives did not have a language but dialects, it was assumed that they did not have culture. In this way those who have power profile those who don't have power. From a certain moment of the experience those who don't have power accept the profile determined by the dominant. When the dominated begin to struggle they reject the profile, this is why the blacks in the 1960s cried out to the world that "black is beautiful." It was a way the blacks had to reject the profile of the ugliness of blacks as determined by the dominant white.

Creating solidarity among those who are different but have somewhat the same kind of dream implies admitting different understandings of the profile of the dream. The question comes to the domain of objectivity not subjectivity, and the struggle includes some work on understanding and dealing with these problems, on creating strategies, on working on respect for the differences. At any rate, I think that first of all they should work on the possibility of becoming solidary and not against one another.

For me the question of solidarity is, therefore, a political question and is also a methodological question. It has to do with the preparation for reaching the dream. Your question was very good. Without exploring it I might have hidden in my answers something very important. Thank you.

Q: *The other element is that in addition to being a question, the professor also has to be a witness, a testimony, so that when the student expresses himself or herself with frustration, the professor also has to show himself in his frustration. So, in addition to hope, critical mind, and solidarity, there is also a witnessing testimony that you have to provide to make all of this possible.*

PF: Yes, very good. I think we all agree. The teacher must be a question who embodies and becomes a testimony. Personally, it justifies for me having come to the states just for this morning. The nature of the other meetings was different, this is one of the best experiences that I have ever had. Thank you very much.

This dialogical seminar convened, by invitation, an interdisciplinary group of scholars, who collaborated for a few months in advance and finally met with Paulo Freire, at the University of Northern Iowa. The group, organized by Christopher Edginton and Walter de Oliveira (UNI), included Nick Ashwell (University of Reading, England), Michael Baizerman (University of Minnesota), Sarah Banks (Durham University, England), Joe Levy (Atkinson College), James McPherson (University of Iowa), Norman Sprinthall (North Carolina State University), Jerry Stein (in outreach community service, Minneapolis, MN), Bruce Thomas (Children's Learning Project, Chicago), plus UNI professors Carmen Montecinos, Peggy Ishler, Roger Sell, Robert Krueger, Bob Muffoletto, and Gretta Berghammer.

Chapter 4

For a Pedagogy of Solidarity

Walter Ferreira de Oliveira

To doubt what is right and not what is questionable,
here is wisdom.

Celestin Freinet

Fatalism and Compliance: Pedagogy of Oppression

Paulo Freire's work repeatedly invites us to reflect on the identity of
the educational process. It is not uncommon in our society to hold a
vision of education strictly as a set of learning mechanisms with their
valuation strongly linked to the formal, and valued usually only when it
is education "acquired" at school—the courses offered by formally ac-
credited educational institutions. But, from Freire's view the educational process is much more than the knowledge acquired didactically in formal institutions. Education is for him a key to the management of our
own dilemma of human existence, a transcendent phenomenon—both
a tool and a field of creation. It can be used as an adaptation scheme or
can be exercised as a locus of personal maturation, which involves the
exchange of knowledge and the creation of a social dynamic for building

Pedagogy of Solidarity, Paulo Freire, Ana
Maria Araújo Freire, and Walter de Oliveira.
© 2014 by Ana Maria Araújo Freire and
Walter Ferreira de Oliveira, pp. 65–84.

new knowledge. In this sense, education is an epiphenomenon, a reflection of the cultural, social, and political through interpersonal relationships, communities and institutions.

Education is thus a transforming agent of these structures. It is not a neutral activity, but a territory of development and mobilization where intense clashes and conflicts are experienced. The question of identity is intertwined with the teaching of the fundamental questions of epistemology. Melvin Rader (1976) helps us to locate these questions: "How do we know? How can we know? How do we know this? How can we distinguish between appearance and reality? What is the nature of the truth and how do we distinguish what is true from what is false?" This approach includes education with, in the words of Rader "undying issues," the main problems of philosophy, the questions that insist on not being ignored.

To examine human existence in its knowledge, structures, interrelations, intricacies, nuances, and idiosyncrasies; to decipher meanings, symbolism, representations, and practices; and to study societies, forms of association between people, organizations, movements, and institutions as well as models, paradigms, and ways of life, this is the crux of education, and it can be considered the heart of the social sciences and humanities. The object of education is the study of the system of relationships, human and environmental, whose balance and harmonization is defined by the conjunction and application of knowledge.

For the inevitably central object of study of these relationships one returns to education and pedagogical processes. Our institutions, our professional actions, our customs, and much of our mental life are conditioned by social and educational processes experienced in school environments—vocational and academic—as well as through social and educational structures external to formal education. Most of these educational relationships take place informally, in the context of social and cultural influences that also constitute teaching and function as shared teaching and learning.

The analysis of this social and cultural process we call education triggers knowledge beyond the technical and expands the universe of knowledge. It allows us, for example, to understand the importance of intuitive knowledge, the exercise of criticism, and the balance between subjectivity and objectivity as fundamental necessities for the constant renewal of knowledge. This understanding of education reveals a horizon that presents a fundamental theme—the reading of the world, how we come to know this world, and the ways we relate to this world. And, this way of approaching the world's knowledge, the awareness of our being in the world, drives us because of our human vocation toward the desire for transformation.

This analysis based on Freire, which is always current, reveals itself as a civilizing action of the highest degree, in that it contributes to socio-educational projects and their profound impact on human progress, but not without causing deep discomfort in the current historical moment. We face the undeniable establishment of a historic crisis, now widely seen in the work of Paulo Freire and many other social commentators, including Boaventura de Sousa Santos, Edgar Morin, Zygmunt Bauman, Leonardo Boff, José Saramago, Jean Baudrillard, Peter McLaren, Henry Giroux, Donaldo Macedo, Anthony Giddens, Jürgen Habermas, Hannah Arendt, and Teixeira Coelho. On the face of it this crisis is manifested in the tendency toward fragmentation and disordered knowledge, the tacit acceptance of superficiality, the institutional arrangements in favor of the average over the pursuit of excellence and transcendence, the rejection of proposed amendments to the path set by the prevailing economic power, the intolerance toward questions that challenge the existence of and are proposed in the context of this cultural-economic structure.

In the midst of this historic crisis, it is argued that the subjugation to an epistemologically illusory objectivism is a direct child of the most reactionary aspects of positivism. It has called for the organization of livelihoods based on a supposed science based primarily on market economic order, a science that guides educational institutions to produce and market supply to serve the interests of the market. That science would, in principle, abolish the criticisms that can effectively suggest structural changes. Freire (1996) shows us that this crisis is based on a historical fatalism whose argumentative strategy is guided by the present way of life subjugated to the ideology of the market as the only possibility for social development and as the only way to achieve prosperity and manipulate the powerful illusions of security and happiness.

A fundamental principle guides this unique path proposed by the ideology of the market: the transformation of all things, inanimate or living, into elements subject to commodification. Nature—water, air, outer space, land, forests—and humans and all other beings, their labor, their bodies, their minds, their feelings, their sexuality, their beauty, their knowledge, their consciences, their homes, and their lives are considered as commodities. Everything and everyone is for sale; everything and everyone must have its price. The realization of this (sacred) view is determined through some well-known ideological and organizational principles, including the valuation of fundamental profit; competitiveness as a way of organizing relations; privileging the private over the public, and large corporations over all; a liberal attitude in relation to the flow of capital, goods, and services linked to these corporations; the dominance of economics as a field organizer of socio-political relations; the weakening of the protective and regulatory functions of the state; the maximum exploitation of labor; the destruction of protective institutions for work, including the unions; and strong encouragement of individualism and accumulation of goods. Each of these principles demands action strategies and operational modes that strengthen and materialize through standards, processes, and daily activities performed by individuals, groups, and institutions.

The final implementation of the way of life governed by the market is a historical enterprise, organized from highly complex joint international, national, and local efforts, and supported by extremely sophisticated behavior control systems. The market needs people to identify themselves not only as human beings, but as consumers who lose their scruples in the scheme of competitiveness, leaving the social ethics of solidarity behind to believe in profit as the higher value. It is still necessary that certain principles of economics, such as efficiency, interpreted in the manner most convenient to this ideology, are accepted as natural guiding principles of public policy. The market especially needs people, even if they do not fully accept the ways of life that are offered, who believe there is no alternative or better social system, or that they cannot change this reality.

This historical fatalism is based on a broad political production wish in a psychology focused on the manufacture of certain forms of relationships, the corruption of the political and judicial powers, and the co-opting of social institutions and intellectual leaders. This set of techniques of social control must be exercised from instruction of the masses that brings with it the conception of human beings as *Homo economicus* and society as a whole as people and relationships with mercantile purposes only.

In this conception of the human proposition and way of life the *invisible hand of the market,* supported by an always healthy competitiveness, exerts a positive regulatory influence that offsets the natural tendency to social breakdown by tackling the impediments to progress toward social and human development as defined in the writings of neoliberal capitalism. Material accumulation and profit are, in this mosaic, the core values of existence in engines of progress of individuals, families, communities, and nations. With this justification, is engendered a subliminally macro-process educational system with the purpose of transmission, acceptance, and absorption of this set of values and beliefs with their subsequent elaborations, prescriptions, and behaviors.

The necessary educational enterprise tor the fatalistic project of promotion and consolidation of life as a subsidiary of market ideology is, therefore, a political-pedagogical process that affects the social field of formal education, shapes the means of mass communication, and permeates informal structures of the most diverse natures. In addition to the institutional mechanisms, this venture grows through human relations—communal and social—in socio-educational powers that Canclini (1998) refers to as the discredited powers. Those beliefs, mandates, laws, norms, which pervade all levels of relationships, enter homes; influence the relationships of neighbors in the neighborhood and commercial transactions of all types; and affect ways of being and conduct, and the understanding of social roles within the family, civic life, and existence as a whole.

This sociopolitical scheme of the social-pedagogical psychology oriented to social cultural control has traditionally been used in the historical search for aggregation of thoughts and habits, such as in Nazi Germany and Fascist Italy, and today is, with the technology available, taken to degrees of extreme sophistication. One of the possible consequences of socio-pedagogy is that, from the fatalistic submission to the values, beliefs, and norms of behavior and interpretations of reality offered by the neoliberal ideology of the market, a sense of doubt is lost, along with the argumentation and discussion that allow us to dream, visualize, discover, experience, create, and establish other ways of understanding the existence and manifestation of the human vocation. Thus, the political pedagogical project market for human existence has propositions, objectives, strategies, tactics, and operations well defined with respect to its ideological, moral, psychological, and social dimensions. The hand may be partially invisible, but it does not act in any way by chance.

Pedagogical Proposals in Conflict:
Conformism versus Humanization

The whole package of social control that comes via the social-pedagogical includes the preaching of total subservience—complete, indisputable, and inexorable cultural submission to the ideological structure of the market—and has as a corollary the mechanization and dehumanization of human beings. This topic has been extensively explored in the social sciences and humanities since the first half of the twentieth century by a number of authors, including Erich Fromm (1955), Paul Tillich (1952), Rollo May (1972), and R. D. Laing (1967). In their analyses, the process of dehumanization due to oppression was located more clearly as a result of the division of classes by economic categories or by membership in categories identified as minorities of power, as in the case of discrimination on the basis of race, gender, or mental condition (Fanon 1963; Friedan, 1963, Knowles & Prewitt, 1969; Szasz. 1970). In the analysis of the phenomenon of social exclusion can be seen more clearly the issues of social inequality and the different forms of suffering reduced to differences in economic class or categories of social power.

Freire (1970) was one of the first to relativize this analysis, pointing out the phenomenon of identification with the oppressed and the oppressor's bias when their reality of oppression is altered and they assume the identity of the oppressor. He showed, as Viktor Frankl (1963) had already warned, that not only can other oppressed classes and categories be affected, but members of the same class or category can move from the position of submission, to that of the oppressor when given the opportunity through purchasing power.

Today one of our perplexities involves the growing number of people who, although they do not directly feel the hardships of poverty and they are not classified in categories traditionally seen as the oppressed, display a broad spectrum of social vulnerability. The analysis of that vulnerability has long been ignored in the knowledge structure and even sometimes ridiculed among intellectuals and the labor "left" because they understand that you cannot compare the suffering of the poor with that of the bourgeoisie and the small bourgeoisie. But, we are increasingly led to realize that now there is, at some level, a suffering common to human beings as a whole, one that transcends membership in a class and social category. This does not in any way mean that social classes no longer exist or that the privileged and the middle classes have the same degree of suffering as the socially and economically disadvantage. It is very difficult to imagine the measurement of suffering, but it can be said that people have different ways to experience and express grief. The fact is that today we can increasingly find dehumanization of victims—the brutality, violence, and savagery that characterize the current historical crisis—in all segments of society in proportion. As stated by Freire in *Pedagogy of the Oppressed*, oppression dehumanizes everyone, oppressors and oppressed, and opposes the human vocation of humanization.

In the context of universal oppression is established a reality dominated by the "mechanization" of the human being. This reality is clearer at work where the complete and utter exploitation of labor is seen in the socio-pedagogical neoliberal scheme as perfectly normal. Also standard is to facilitate this exploitation with job insecurity when facing the capital, that is, the weakening of workers at any level against corporate profit goals. For this to take effect, you need to make relationships impersonal, that is to say, take away the human characteristics of the people, seeing them not as human beings but as "human capital" or "manpower"—designations that mitigate the actions to be taken in favor of unemployment, cutting benefits, and flattening wages. In addition, space is precarious and space requirements increasingly inhumane, and the establishment of goals and objectives increasingly harmful to the health and dignity of workers at various levels, from factory workers to bank managers, from university professors to telecommunications workers.

Mediators of the values of transactions relating to the production and distribution of goods and services are also taken to the level of dehumanization. For example, the production of durable goods and real estate speculation involved in the stimulating of demand for and increasing the supply of energy with the establishment of a complex electromagnetic transmission system using equipment harmful to health and potentially harmful to the environment are justified by the growing economy and increased job opportunities. Sales of products become opportunities for persuasion or deception, or to convince neighbors to take risks, incur liabilities, or make commitments that may result in their unhappiness or their ruin. These are justified as the attempt of the seller to fulfill a professional obligation that arises as a plus point for career success.

Dehumanizing values typical of the relations between labor and production are recognized in other types of relationships, such as regulatory human transactions in other environments. Dehumanization is promoted and enhanced in these environments through radical stimulus to competitiveness, individualism, and selfishness. One consequence is the estrangement between people who see themselves as potential adversaries or as potential means for achieving each other's objectives. Relations are to be based on fear, suspicion, and material interest. This existential proposal clearly manifested in the workplace and often repeated in propaganda from other socio-pedagogical environments, causes hopelessness and loss of meaning in life for many. This can be worse for those whose social and economic position is more vulnerable, those whose vicissitudes and precarious levels of "disempowerment" hinder the establishment of a social and psychological need to overcome this brutal reality.

Therefore, this fundamental dilemma posed by Freire in *Pedagogy of the Oppressed* more than forty years ago is still the most important axiomatic issue regarding the viability of society—the problem of humanization. The issue is crucial though inescapably undesirable from the point of view of the currently hegemonic capitalist powers since the fatalistic ideology of the market bases its existence on dehumanization.

The historical moment shows therefore a clear cultural and epistemological clash. The market requires the brutalization and destruction of the sense of community; the transmutation of living spaces—cities, streets, houses—earth, water, air, bodies, people, work, and life into goods; and the taking away of individual and population characteristics that serve to realize and complete any project compatible with a human vocation that is not mechanization. The market ideology demands the "objectification" of the people, who are to be treated as disposable objects easily replaced, which in turn facilitates their exploitation as labor that is increasingly devalued. This ideological stance requires a maximum of ephemeral human relations, fragile and poorly conducted, and always places suspicion on movements and forms of union that can become the seeds of troublesome questions. The strengthening of this ideology needs to devalue and disrespect life. This devaluation and disrespect culminate in the disregard for other human beings evident in the violence plaguing the planet like an epidemic of horrific proportions. Another side effect is the disregard for other living beings and nature in general, both of which are now also perceived as "economic resources," thus an anthropocentrism that is leading to the destruction of the environment and of life itself.

The ideologists of the market, however, live a paradox that can be described as follows: "theater history" where social demands preserve in any human endeavor, even war, an aura of civilization. Therefore, the design of the market cannot show its real face; it has to appear as the best option for democracy and humanization. To deal with this problem the market ideologues invent compensatory projects, presenting illusory solutions to the problems raised in the context of their biological and social unsustainability. Usually these projects appropriate the languages identified with the antithesis—human environmental and social sustainability—which complicates and confuses the discussion of these issues. This is what happens, for example, with the very theme of humanization, and with other issues such as solidarity and social responsibility.

Thus, on the one hand, there is the need of the market ideologues to convince, through a pedagogy of the masses, that the way of life proposed by the market society is best for humans. At the same time, for strategic reasons, it must proclaim that there is no other way out, there is no better option. On the other hand, those who do not believe, do not accept and will not submit to these proposals, try to resist through the consolidation of a social pedagogy to submit alternative proposals to the fatalistic pedagogy oriented to the market. This conflict is presented axiomatically around the theme of humanization.

A major complication in this clash is exactly the fact that market ideologues cannot fully reveal their true ideological identity, which leads to the use of a language that misleads their opponents. This ends up seriously damaging public discussion because there is always, from those who do not accept the ideology of the market, the need for clarification of its language, symbols and meanings. As a result, those who are against the ideology of hungry market power are in search of a different language that ends up at some point also being co-opted. Therefore, we see great efforts to create, recreate, or refine concepts and denominations, such as the device of saying we are talking about a "real" humanization, a "true" solidarity, or a "real "social responsibility, and so on. In the end, the confusion is fully harnessed to foster a high degree of uncertainty in public and thus force a conservative choice: "it is better than the chaos that would surely come with the changes." The ideology of market demand thus prevents people from breaking with the historical fatalism that it seeks to promote.

It seems, therefore, highly necessary in the current context to have a public discussion informed by the significance of the idea of humanization taken as a central problem for the viability of contemporary society. And, as a result, a discussion of the main pedagogical mechanisms that either indicate a facilitation of or an increasing destruction of the humanization process. It brings to the agenda, in this sense, the question of solidarity.

The Education of the Twenty-first Century: The Place of Humanization and Solidarity

In one of the texts in this book, Paulo Freire argues with various thinkers about how education should be in the twenty-first century. He permeates this discussion, directly and indirectly, with the issue of humanization and, as a corollary, solidarity. Clearly, when discussing the pedagogy of the neighborhood, relationships with one another, and the role of hope—central themes in his work—he speaks to the depth and transcendence, to opportunities, choices, and how these opportunities and choices present themselves before the most representative component of the human vocation, which is manifested n *Pedagogy of the Oppressed* and *Pedagogy of Hope* (1995) as humanization, which goes against the dehumanization.

Regarding solidarity, in *Pedagogy of the Oppressed* Freire distinguishes charity, which is not considered by him as solidarity, from another true solidarity, which is assistance provided to you that you need, so that you will no longer need. Solidarity in this sense is to share the struggle of trying to escape various forms of oppression. It is a manifestation of support and existential posture and policy. To share the fight against the oppression of the other is to join this other in achieving social justice; it is to go beyond the limits of charity to provide an eventual help that is assumed to be a liberating action.

Solidarity can also be defined by its operational characteristics, in other words in the way it can manifest itself concretely. It materializes amidst the struggles between the oppressed and the oppressors at different levels. These struggles are more visible when considering political movements, but can also be found in less obvious situations, such as everyday relationships in work or home life, in the use of public and private services, in the abuses of power that are presented daily before ordinary citizens. Being supportive at this situational level is often not an attitude directed at an individual person. We can even be in solidarity with people with whom we are not in direct contact, because we face common problems. We sympathize when we share the struggle against situations of abuse or in resistance to the decisions that others make; we are setting up solidarity as a fluid dynamic that goes beyond the personal connection.

These forms of solidarity are representative of the struggles of groups that suffer oppression in a piecemeal manner, such as junior officials persecuted by oppressive leaders; in the situation we now call bullying; children subjected to abuse in homes, schools, and shelters; elderly victims of abuse; consumers dealing with standards and regulations that serve as a subterfuge to prevent them from demanding quality standards for products and services; public or private persons who, by their condition of difference are labeled as sexual minorities; people with mental disorders; former prisoners; those fighting hegemonic ideologies at their level in universities; and members of organizations defending the environment All of these situations are important variables for how a society behaves as a whole and cannot fail to be addressed in an education properly inserted into the project of being a nation and being humanity. The fundamental question is how to ensure that current and future citizens have access, in schools and through a socio-pedagogical reaching out, a knowledge of these issues that equips one for critical analysis. In addressing this issue we should be concerned about how to achieve this without falling into the same mistake of trying to use the formal education of the masses as a mere means of indoctrination.

It is, therefore, necessary to think of practical ways to approach the major issues related to building a just, humane, and supportive environment for the development of people as citizens. Edgar Morin (1997), echoing Freire, proposes that the smartest way to do it is by turning to the idea of community. Morin argues that the resumption of a community spirit, which he feels is lost but recoverable, is essential for social sustainability. He makes sense, since we live in a social complex where systems and subsystems, groups, individuals, families, businesses, and institutions direct and constantly influence each other, creating what we call social life.

A posture of radical individualism in which each person worries primarily about their own problems without regard to others, is a sure path to social disintegration. The notion of community life, which includes respect, concern for others, and solidarity, is, in this sense, fundamental. The relationship between solidarity and community presents itself as direct and inescapable. We must then follow our reasoning and seek the inclusion of these notions in the education of contemporary human beings in how to strengthen community spirit.

A need to strengthen the community and study its meaning is to live it as experience. Community cannot be understood without a community practice. Community life is relative and therefore cannot only be contained in theorizing, any theories that are presented for analysis must be accompanied by a lively practice, manifested not as academic observations, but in the community's very existence. In this sense, an education that contributes to strengthening the community, and thus to social progress, has to be immersed in community life. This notion is not new. In the first half of the twentieth century, Freinet (1969/1947) and Freire himself (1970) promoted experiments where the educational process and school were part of the community context, experiences that fully demonstrated its success, but unfortunately, for ideological reasons, these education plans were abolished in subsequent governments. Already in the 1980s the experience of Street Social Education (Oliveira, 2004) again demonstrated the strength of an educational project aimed at training citizens in the community context. These educational forms need to be resumed and retrofitted. Their theoretical frameworks and reports of practices can be of immense use to the sustainable progress of our civilization, which so needs educationally healthy experiences .

Thus, the insertion of humanization and solidarity on the one hand and the strengthening of community living on the other are fundamental elements of the educational process and constitute a major challenge for education in the twenty-first century. Without these elements present and vigorously active, it becomes more difficult for a social project that guarantees human sustainability.

A society that provides humane conditions for sustainable human and humanization design must include solidarity if we define this as a link between people, a sincere concern for each other, that allows the development of a concrete group spirit, a social body of community life. In this sense, social progress is a direct function of the degree of solidarity between its various members, whether they are considered as individuals, groups, or categories.

Solidarity is a cohesive force that facilitates the functioning community and social life. This view is opposed to the idea of solidarity as a mere synonym for charity, whose nature is compensatory, seeking to correct the consequences of social projects seen as evil, such as the unfair distribution of wealth, the devaluation of life, and social inequality. Solidarity is a positive construction and can inspire the creation of structural mechanisms that avoid the need for further compensation.

Education for personal, social, and environmental sustainability should therefore be humanizing, fomenting solidarity and empowering community. For this it has to face the historical fatalism of market ideology that preaches the radical extreme individualism and competitiveness that is directly opposed to humanization and solidarity, interpreting the latter as charity and philanthropy. The neoliberal fatalism needs the "mechanization" and "technification" of human beings and the weakening or destruction of the community; it is essentially fragmentary, disruptive, and dissociative.

Several attempts have been made at various levels to create effective forms of education that are more humane and compassionate, with varying degrees of success. Some specific initiatives include pedagogy subdivision; critical pedagogy of place in the United States; the community education found in some European countries; work with children and youth (Youthwork) and social education, which had their heyday in the 1990s and are latent in the United States, Europe, and Latin America; as well as projects currently in vogue in Brazil under the name popular education. These initiatives suffer from the fundamental problem of the artificial separation between school and non-formal education, an issue that should be further explored in other opportunities.

An interesting model of state educational action that tries to deconstruct this fragmentation is that of community colleges in the United States. This model is an attempt to put together a formal structure, usually large, with an education geared towards professionalism, while providing a meeting ground between training and use of community services. The model follows the American tradition of community participation in political and pedagogical processes that was initiated in the nineteenth century with community schools according to the teachings of Colonel Parker. Another lively and interesting project is to put the community into discussions about building its own destiny with a funding initiative for community centers and their variants, such as social centers for youth for the third age, for other sections of the population, and for users of psychiatric services and the like. This model is common in Europe and also has an important application in countries such as Cuba, Colombia, Mexico, Australia, New Zealand, and South Africa

From the point of view of the theoretical and practical (and Freire, Freinet and Street Social Education as already mentioned) is social pedagogy as promoted by Anton Makarenko in Russia and the Soviet Union, which is another important source of inspiration, incorporating the socio-pedagogical provided by productive activities and the media of mass communication. Of course, when dealing with productive activities related to education, such as the U. S. community colleges, Freinet schools popular in France, or the production of goods promoted by Makarenko, there is the danger of falling, once again, into the orientation for a professional education vision that is essentially marketing, where the goal is not the process of integration into production as a means of teaching experience and community, but only the product, the result, the good or service that is offered. This type of problem is lived intensely, for example, in the workshops that flourish in institutions where specific groups are trained for processes to generate income. One of the challenges of these educational processes is to balance the pursuit of quality of products with the dynamics of the process, making the activity not only a means of producing income, but also a means of personal growth and a chance to increase the degree of humanization, solidarity, and social inclusion.

In the Guise of Conclusion

The education needed to advance dehumanization is an education for dressage. This type of education, fought by Paulo Freire and masterfully debunked by Paula Brugger (1994), is now promoted globally and reaches full strength and sophistication with a new face in the peripheral countries. This education project is contextualized by the scrapping of public services and social safety nets, strengthened by a media that lies between myopia and partiality, and driven by corrupt governments subservient to the design or delivery of public assets for the use of dead institutions, domestic and international.

But despite a framework favorable to dehumanization and despair, the voices of some thinkers join the undying hope of educators who refuse to simply line up for this collective project of miseducation. For them it is worthwhile, as Paulo Freire says, to still and always be dreaming, to speak in ideals and utopias, and to think of ways to achieve them. For this doubt, As Freinet suggests, we must doubt not only what is clearly dubious, but also that which we would try to impose as absolute truths.

That is why we reject this "absolute truth" that some would try to enforce, that subservience to market ideology will bring us happiness, that environmental destruction is inevitable, and that it is good we yield to the forces of imperialist capital speculation. We must vehemently reject the transformation of education as dressage, which is just one more way to domesticate humans, to make them uncritical labor, and naive slaves to ventures that would result in their own destruction. We must defend at all levels an education that is critical, humanizing, supportive, and empowering of community spirit, and believe that education is essential to the well-being of the wider population. We believe that social justice is possible and that we can in practice promote it. For this we have to want to learn and work, knowing that there is another process in action promoting not wanting to unlearn, allied to the promotion of alienated labor, and suffering the inertia of paralyzing and overwhelming social movements, and that, with Freire, we refuse to accept this.

Chapter 5

Testimony of Difference and the Right to Discuss Difference

Some Considerations on Paulo Freire's Conference

Ana Maria Araujo Freire

When we decided to write this book, Walter de Oliveira and I thought it would be important for each of us to comment on Paulo's presentations in Cedar Falls, Iowa. We both participated in those presentations and we thought we should say something about what Paulo said on those memorable days in the heartland of the United States shortly before he passed away. These reflections of mine, then, are motivated by that goal, although Walter claims the right to greater flexibility over his comments on Paulo's work than I do.

Starting from my feelings and memories and from my husband's words written on a piece of paper that translate, as always, the concreteness of what he felt, did, thought, and spoke, I am going to offer my comments. I intend to call the attention of Paulo's readers to some elements of his first conference at the University of Northern Iowa, emphasizing some of his thoughts and adding important information about his ethical-pedagogical posture. This is my critical analysis of his speech.

First, I need to explain my choice for the title of this book—*Pedagogy of Solidarity* (Pedagogia da solidariedade). I chose this not only because

Pedagogy of Solidarity, Paulo Freire, Ana Maria Araújo Freire, and Walter de Oliveira. © 2014 by Ana Maria Araújo Freire and Walter Ferreira de Oliveira, pp. 85–98.

Paulo spoke emphatically in his talk about this necessary virtue for the construction of a democratic society in the works, and not only because of my own considerations, but also because it reflects the beliefs of the others in this book. It emphasizes Paulo's own solidarity practice, intensively lived in its most authentic meaning.

From his Catholic education, Paulo brought some influences to his educational thinking, theological virtues among others. However, I must say, these virtues were overcome by ethical-political-pedagogical categories in his understanding of education and in its praxis. From theology, we can easily see the virtues of:

- faith, which he reformulated according to an unshakeable faith in men and women;

- hope, which acquired a new meaning before his comprehension of human incompleteness and of the ability to dream of utopia in the sense of making possible the being more, to make real human existence true;

- charity, which became solidarity, solidarity with the world and with earth's sustainability, for it involves profound solidarity with all men and women of the world.

My first consideration is to alert the readers of this book that Paulo was not repetitive when talking about his favorite subjects, even the ones he most commonly addressed. He used different approaches to problems that troubled him at the time of his speeches, or problems that he was asked by his peers to speak of. His words, even if they sound familiar, speak differently about what he had already said and written, since "copying himself" is something he never did, due to his incredible ability to create and recreate. Filled with an exuberant imagination, Paulo never took advantage of what other people said or wrote without quoting them. However, being as creative as he was—a volcano, as Claudius Ceccon emblematically portrayed his head[1]—maybe Paulo quoted less than what "careful" academics require from authors.

Paulo's creative exuberance is due to the absence of prejudice, his openness to new worlds, and his permanent love regarding living beings and their way of being. To his good humor and nonconformity, his taste for rebellion and denial of accommodation, and his attitude of indignation, persistence and dedication we can attribute his daily struggle for a better world.

Paulo's creative exuberance was also due to many other qualities and virtues, including the epistemological curiosity that drove him to observe, search, find, compare, study, and reflect all day long, reading the world and the words of the most diverse thinkers. From these he formulated his own words. His harshest critics never understood from where so many ideas flowed. That is why many still accuse him, unfairly, of not identifying where he got his ideas and which authors were his sources. He sought his ideas by reading others, but fundamentally his ideas came from his own insightful ability to find truths with his intuition and common sense, in his daily experiences and observations of the obvious things on which he focused his thinking. He did his own critical thinking.

Paulo's words sound familiar because, as always, he insisted on fundamental themes of his pedagogical theory—criticism, ethics, politics, liberation—which he believed were absolutely necessary to be said over and over. He problematized thematic issues that he continuously raised in similar but different ways to give concreteness to untested feasibilities,[2] highlighted by his lucidity, subtlety, and wit. For Paulo "retelling" had the meaning and intention of continually reformatting his ideas because he focused on the object to be unveiled, known by the many different angles by which he thought that they should be analyzed or rigorously addressed in different historical moments and cultural sites.

I also draw readers' attention to the fact that he did not repeat in this Iowa conference the paths of cognoscibility, of how to address issues, as he usually did. He treated them in an innovative way, always adding something more, greatly concerned with ethics and aesthetics every time he did so. He did not mechanically repeat his answers to the challenges posed to him. He treated each one of them in the same fashion as those who asked the question—subjectively, but without neglecting objectivity. He demanded of himself both a scientific rigor and an ethical-sociopolitical focus, without forgetting his pedagogical and aesthetic concerns. He did not repeat themes to fill the time in reverie without direction, he went straight to the issues that plague us as beings *in* the world, unveiling them from several different angles.

Paulo always chose the lush and fertile path of politics, love, and dialogue. He had done so since his youth, and persisted even in this conference, while living fully the wisdom of his intellectual and personal maturity. He spoke poetically, elaborated with an aesthetic rigor, looking for the liberation of all. From the ethic of life so radical in which he himself was immersed, true energy emanated from his authentic humanism, from his belief that the supreme good of human existence is *life* itself. Life with dignity. Life built in democracy.

Early on the evening of March 24, 1996, Paulo stood with his usual simplicity and humility absorbing the words of high praise from Bob Koob, president of the University of Northern Iowa, and from Brazilian professor Walter de Oliveira. He kept himself calm and at ease in front of an audience full of students and teachers, some of them protesting his dialectical way of composing ideas and his progressive ideas.

Much more than other speeches he had made, this address of Paulo's—a testimony of difference and the right to discuss difference—

exposed his dialectical experience of continuously asking himself, and asking us, not to unfold his own experiences. It demonstrates the authentic, progressive coherence that we watched, lived, felt, systematized, wrote, and spoke.

He began humbly, saying about his words, "I always, in circumstances like this, ask myself, what will I speak about?" He entered the space generator of things, his epistemological curiosity, wondering, asking those who listened with attention and respect, and establishing dialogue. Strictly dialectical—Paulo was always so, even as a person—he showed the audience the relationship between the nature of humanity and history, a history that produced us and that we produce, stating "as historical beings we are constantly engaged in the creation and recreation of our own nature."

So, without forgetting "history" and "culture," Paulo raised the question of experience, denied by academics as unreliable in the light of scientific rigor. Paulo always took great care and warned us about the limits of science, to not invade the culture of other people, because he considered this unacceptably disrespectful, a political and philosophical mistake as well as a cultural misunderstanding. It was clear in his critical consciousness that educational and other experiences are not transferred, moved, or repeated. Doing so is to deny the historicity and culture of the other, the different. Hence he always refused to redo or repeat the dynamics and tactics of education as practiced so successfully before the Brazilian coup of 1964 in popular culture movements—Popular Culture Movement (MCP) and others—or in the National Literacy Program (PNA), which required from us more than mere participation. His was a responsible and a political-pedagogical commitment. With this conviction of the importance of this conference, he said: "education develops in history, in history it is born and becomes historically, as we build ourselves not only historically and genetically." Paulo never had pretensions of exporting our experiences from Brazil in the 1960s to any other part of the world, nor to repeat them after his return to his own country.

I consider it important to draw attention to the metaphors that Paulo used at this conference: *soggy* and *wet*. I will appropriate these terms to strengthen my comments on his talk. He boldly stated: "The responsible people for education should be fully wet by the waters of the cultural moment and space in which they operate."

In an unusual way and with amazing beauty, he raised the question of human inconclusiveness that he valued both in himself and in others. Due to the possibilities opened by incompleteness, we fight for hope and the utopia "of a world where it is easier to love." We make *being more* a permanent process: "So that we, human beings, can be what we are, we need to become, to be what we are. We do not need to be—if we simply are, we stop being. We are, precisely because we are becoming." This understanding of inconclusiveness goes beyond the simple "not ready for humans" and gives a dimension of consciousness that allows for a wonderful "adventure," which is the education of each of us as human beings.

Adventure is used in the metaphorical sense of the pursuit of knowledge still unknown, of what can be and still is not, or what already is, but may be different, improved, deepened. Adventure is understood as the moment of spontaneous curiosity that becomes epistemological— that this, truly in its epistemological process, expands and deepens— because it has philosophical and scientific bases in education, liberating the formation of daring citizenship and autonomy. Adventure is understood as a time of amazement and marvel. Thus, creative acts *bathed* in possible dreams—and we make tomorrow possible by fighting today—of the untold possibilities of things to do with ethical education and policy that respect cultures, with subjectivity and objectivity of the philosophical, scientific, or religious. Adventure in the field of knowledge needs to be unveiled, seized, learned, lived and communicated, never extended or imposed.

Paulo subtly highlighted the difference between *possibility* and *reality*: "One of human beings' characteristics is the ability to venture and one of the nicest things is taking risks." This risk-taking as *beauty* is implicit in the adventure of knowing and living with responsibility.

The adventure that Paulo proposed does not fit being spontaneous or irresponsible, nor does it fit rote prescriptions, *banking education*, elitism, discrimination, oppression, and exclusion. These are the "make-believe" of irresponsible people. So is the virtual world and its evil created from technological development in the service of neoliberalism and globalization. It is rather the *humanist adventure* that gives us the joy and pleasure of meeting, knowing, and living to serve everyone, and not just an individual's appropriation to serve dilettantism and the selfishness of the owners of the world. Paulo's is an adventure with decency, dignity, and respect, with tolerance, love, and rigor. It is an adventure that enables us to nourish our utopia, our dreams of better and more democratic days.

Believing and testifying in the ongoing process of renewal and creation, Paulo never asked anybody to be his disciple, to follow him. Instead, he always asked them to outperform him, recreating his ideas in a better form. Whoever only speaks and acts in a way that follows the Master and repeats him diminishes Freire's ideas! "If you follow me, you destroy me," he said at the conference, emphasizing what he would always say with conviction, claiming an anthropological, ethical, historical, social, and political truth.

On this point I have something important to say, to alert readers. It is common to find ideas, works, or events, many of them truly inconsequential aberrations, for which the authors claim shamelessly and categorically, "I'm recreating Paulo Freire." Recreating does not distort,

deform, and turn the original creator of these ideas deliberately prag-
matic. Neither does it minimize and diminish the sayings, writings, and
deeds of another, in this case Paulo. When recreating, it is necessary
to ethically and responsibly respect what is absolutely essential in the
statements, writings, and deeds of the person who is being copied. We
have to respect the thought and attitude of the original ideas. In Paulo's
case, understanding the fundamentals of his critical-ethical-political
education, his theory of humanistic knowledge, and his stance toward
humanizing in favor of the oppressed are all essential ingredients for
anyone who wishes to recreate his work. Above all, it is aligned with his
loving and respectful generosity.

In the second stage of his Iowa speech Paulo invited us to try "an
exercise of critical reflection." He then moved the focus away from his
critical thinking on educational status by enumerating its constituent
elements. On each one of them, he posed a rationale of scientific and
epistemological arguments, both political and philosophical, returning
synthetically with every new item to that which he had already stated
on other items. In other words, in a very particular and exemplary way,
Paulo made a point to go beyond and return over and over again while
synthesizing what had already been said.

At this conference Paulo did not try to escape from this dialectic-
ally rich path, which is provocative and not always easily understood by
those who do not want to penetrate to the core of his dialectical, complex, and rigorous thinking. He criticized the authoritarian stance of
some educators, exposing the difference between educator and student.
He commented on the distortion of his work that argued there was no
difference between the two parties in the act of educating, emphasizing
that the essence of democratic education, the "beauty of the process [of
education] is exactly this possibility of relearning, exchange" between
these two poles.

Even accepting that assertions without consistency, without criticality, were made to Paulo, naively or maliciously, I consider it important to introduce the issue here to correct this distortion. In Brazil, after his return from exile, given his comment in *Pedagogia do oprimido* that "nobody educates anybody, nobody educates himself, men [and women] are educated by each other, mediated by the world," critics argued that he would have denied the specific role of the act of teaching teachers their proper knowledge, experiences, and reflections thus leaving no difference between the roles of student and teacher. This interpretation was a great mistake in the understanding that the *"conteudistas"* had of my husband's works. They called Paulo an idealist and an inconsequential dreamer.

At this conference Paulo explained his constant search for consistency when someone asks himself: "What does it mean for me to teach?" He went on to add the issue of democracy, ultimately the end of his political and ethical epistemology, as an intrinsic part of liberation and humanization as dreamed by him: "Am I being consistent in my practice with what I think about teaching? For I can think democratically about teaching, but be authoritative in my teaching practice." One cannot be a real educator, a progressive educator if we do not wonder about our attitudes, about our performance, and whom we are for or against. What are we educating for: democracy or the preservation of unfair and perverse structures?

Paulo gave us an explanation on directivity in the educational process, not privileging the political level, as he had commonly been doing, but adding another perspective: "Directivity in education, philosophically and epistemologically understood, means that education is as a process, means something beyond itself....When I say "beyond" this means that education is always related to a dream and that teachers should have their own dreams, their own utopias." Directivity warns us that education does not necessarily mean authoritarianism. Joining the "dream and fight[ing] for your dreams" with the right teacher or educator to speak their dreams, exemplifies and reinforces the directivity of the educational act.

At this conference Paulo pointed out the contradictions of human existence: excesses of authority (authoritarianism) and exaggerated freedom (licentiousness), which he worried more and more about in the last years of his life, above his concerns about the dictates of neoliberalism and how parents educate their sons and daughters today. About this contradictory pair of ideas—authority versus freedom—he remarked profoundly that "authority is an invention of freedom. Freedom invented authority so that freedom could continue to exist."

For this reason Paulo was not afraid to emphasize, even in a crowd of mainly young people, the necessity of example, a historical reality in which the world is understood as mimicry, example, stagnation, and permanence; "things from the old days;" or that "education demands examples, witnesses. He testified to the strength of ideology, challenging the suggestion of its non existence and addressing the question of who's afraid to accept the risk and face the "masters of the world" in not accepting it, among other examples.

Always anxious to make clear their assertions, he constantly made use of the expressions "in other words" and "i.e.," demonstrating his humility and deep desire to be understood. He poeticized their sayings. He faced the challenge with courage, boyishly but not naively saying, "I will die fighting it," i.e., fighting against postmodern fatalist thought dictated by neoliberal economics and globalization. He opposed, as always, puritanism and puritans, vehemently denying their choices in favor of morality and purity.

His speech was permeated with phrases that erased the ethical dilemma of the progressive educator. They must truly want to be beside the lower classes, the oppressed, and the excluded. They must have a clear knowledge of what and for whom, in what and against whom, they teach. There is no neutrality in education. He vehemently reaffirmed the political nature of education. He went beyond that, asserting: "Human existence is a political experience."

To a question from a participant saying that he was following the *banking education* and *extension* methods, depositing knowledge with students and teachers who were present there—a situation "exacerbated" by the arrangement of the chairs in the auditorium placed by the university one behind the other—Paulo tolerantly and calmly replied: "I did not come here to transfer knowledge but to challenge you. . . . And I do not think only about what I have to say, but also about what I am talking about because I establish a contradictory relationship between my speech and my thoughts. For me, this process and the relationship established in this way are different from the banking method."

On this topic, there is a widespread belief, obviously wrong, that for a class to not be considered banking according to Paulo's criteria, everybody should sit in a circle. Only then the teacher would have the physical conditions to teach a lesson that is dialogical and authentically liberating. Looking at the other side, equidistance of each student to his neighbor and to the teacher when all men and women can speak, express their points of view, or ask their questions with equal time for all does not guarantee a classroom in which learning is also socialized. This idealistic and positivist pretense of "equal opportunity for all" does not guarantee in any way the appropriation of affection or distribution without discrimination, it may still be banking education. The issue of geographical space in education is very important, but by itself does not guarantee an inexorable movement toward autonomy and liberation, as indeed Paulo argued in his answer to the student. Autonomy and freedom in a democratic classroom are guaranteed by the relationship of dialogue and lovingness, as Paulo understood it, among those present in the room. The process of autonomy and liberation takes place as part of the pursuit of knowledge.

In saying that, I need to explain what Paulo means by lovingness. It has these connotations in his theory of education:

- the educator must create an affectionate and caring climate in his or her classroom that provides students with the pursuit of knowledge with joy;

- in co-processing without competition among students, the teacher stimulates the adventure of creating and recreating with epistemological curiosity and scientific rigor;

- the educator of necessity has to love the exercise of the educational act; and finally,

- educators have to like the contents of the syllabus of the course they are teaching.

Lovingness does not mean the obligation to love equally all our students, which would be impossible if not hypocritical, but to respect them and care for them with equity.

Paulo affirmed during the conference the "testimony of the difference and the right to discuss the difference" as demonstrated by the boldness, tolerance, and courage to accept differences during his life, the right to discuss a matter within the limits of respect and understanding of its source. "[It] is fantastic that we confuse students" when they have different orientations and different readings of the world from teachers. "You have every right to reject my knowledge and wisdom, to criticize my thinking. But, you have an obligation to respect me and I do not accept being disrespected."

I would like this article to stir readers in order to deepen their first reading so that they can enjoy and better understand what Paulo, with subtlety, clarity, and propriety, proposes to teach us and encourages us to think. If this is not a reader's first reading of Paulo's work, I do not know whether this text of mine will succeed in this goal. For those readers, I admonish them to return to Paulo's writings again and again. Surrender to his words! This is one of the best avenues to learn and grasp the new, deeper, harder truths that Paulo's words instill in us.

In my review I hope to have drawn attention to the testimony of the strength and energy that Paulo deposited in his practice and in his works, clearly visible at this conference. It is meant to enable us to fight against fatalism and for us to believe in the dream that "changing is difficult but it is possible." So, on the day that democracy cannot be more of a utopia—an unprecedented possibility to be built—but reality itself, with men and women humanized and humanizing.

"Do not let this new ideology of fatalism kill your need to dream. Without dreams there is no life, without dreams there is no human being, without dreams there is no human existence."

Notes

1. See the many quotes from Paulo in his works, that contradict this argument, the aforementioned book, chapter 14, 353–364. See the "custody" of Claudius Ceccon in my own book: *Paulo Freire: uma história de vida. Indaiatuba*. Villa das Letras, 2006, awarded with Jabuti Prize, 2007, placed second in the category "The Best Biography Book."
2. Regarding this concept see: Leonardo Boff, Preface, in Paulo Freire, Pedagogia da esperança: um reencontro com a Pedagogia do oprimido, 12th ed. (Rio de Janeiro: Paz e Terra, 2005), n. 1, 205–207; and "Utopia e democracia: os inéditos-viáveis na educação cidadã," in Utopia e democracia na educação cidadã, José Clovis de Azevedo et al, (Porto Alegre: Ed. Universidade/UFRGS/Secretaria Municipal de Educação, 2000).

Chapter 6

The Importance of Pedagogy of Solidarity[1]

Norman K. Denzin

My abhorrence of neoliberalism helps to explain my legitimate anger when I speak of the injustices to which the ragpickers among humanity are condemned. It also explains my total lack of interest in any pretension of impartiality, I am not impartial, or objective . . . [this] does not prevent me from holding always a rigorously ethical position (Freire, 1998, 22).

We each have a responsibility for conducting ethical research that makes a difference in the lives of those whose life opportunities, health, safety, and well-being are diminished by conditions of poverty (Leslie Rebecca Bloom, 2009, 253).

Paulo Freire's *Pedagogy of Solidarity* speaks directly to the role of critical qualitative research in the historical present. The need for social justice has never been greater. Ours is a moment that cries out for emancipatory, pedagogical visions, for visions that inspire transformative inquiries. These are inquiries that provide the moral authority to move people, in their solidarity, to struggle and resist oppression. This will be a model that is broad enough to include work with mining populations in West Virginia, earthquake victims in Haiti, exploited miners in Chile, and

Pedagogy of Solidarity, Paulo Freire, Ana Maria Araújo Freire, and Walter de Oliveira. © 2014 by Ana Maria Araújo Freire and Walter Ferreira de Oliveira, pp. 99–110.

school-age children on American Indian reservations. Paulo's new book leads the way for all of us.

The pursuit of social justice within Paulo's transformative paradigm challenges prevailing forms of inequality, poverty, human oppression, and injustice. This is a pedagogy of solidarity grounded in local neighborhoods. This is a pedagogy that creates new possibilities of experience, while inspiring dreams of hope and utopian possibility. This pedagogy resists the neoliberal drive to create global villages governed by the market system, a system which erases cultural difference. It is grounded in love, forgiveness and joy.

It is a bold pedagogy that is firmly rooted in a human rights agenda. It requires an ethical framework that is rights and social justice based. It requires an awareness of "the need to redress inequalities by giving precedence... to the voices of the least advantaged groups in society" (Mertens, Holmes, & Harris, 2009, 89). It encourages the use of qualitative research for social justice purposes, including making such research accessible for public education, social policymaking, and community transformation.

The desire is to create an ethically responsible agenda that would have these goals:

(1) It places the voices of the oppressed at the center of inquiry;

(2) It uses inquiry to reveal sites for change and activism;

(3) It uses inquiry and activism to help people;

(4) It affects social policy by getting critiques heard and acted on by policy makers;

(5) It affects changes in the inquirer's life, thereby serving as a model of change for others (Bloom and Sawin, 2009, 338, 340–342, 344).

Hope, Pedagogy and the Critical Imagination

As an interventionist ideology the critical imagination is hopeful of change. It seeks and promotes an ideology of hope that challenges and confronts hopelessness (Freire, 1999, 8). It understands that hope, like freedom, is "an ontological need" (Freire, 1999, 8). Hope is the desire to dream, the desire to change, the desire to improve human existence. Hopelessness is "but hope that has lost its bearings" (Freire, 1999, 8).

Hope is ethical. Hope is moral. Hope is peaceful and nonviolent. Hope seeks the truth of life's sufferings. Hope gives meaning to the struggles to change the world. Hope is grounded in concrete performative practices, in struggles and interventions that espouse the sacred values of love, care, community, trust, and well-being (Freire, 1999, 9). Hope as a form of pedagogy confronts and interrogates cynicism, the belief that change is not possible or is too costly. Hope works from rage to love. It articulates a progressive politics that rejects "conservative, neoliberal postmodernity" (Friere, 1999, 10). Hope rejects terrorism. Hope rejects the claim that peace comes at any cost.

The critical democratic imagination is pedagogical, and this in four ways. First, as a form of instruction, it helps persons think critically, historically, sociologically. Second, as critical pedagogy, it exposes the pedagogies of oppression that produce and reproduce oppression and injustice (see Freire, 2001, 54). Third, it contributes to an ethical self-consciousness that is critical and reflexive. It gives people a language and a set of pedagogical practices that turn oppression into freedom, despair into hope, hatred into love, doubt into trust. Fourth, in turn, this self-consciousness shapes a critical racial self-awareness. This awareness contributes to utopian dreams of racial equality and racial justice.

The use of this imagination by persons who have previously lost their way in this complex world is akin to being "suddenly awakened in a house with which they had only supposed themselves to be familiar" (Mills, 1959, 8). They now feel that they can provide themselves with critical understandings that undermine and challenge "older decisions that once appeared sound" (Mills, 1959, 8). Their critical imagination enlivened, persons "acquire a new way of thinking... in a word by their reflection and their sensibility, they realize the cultural meaning of the social sciences" (Mills, 1959, 8). They realize how to make and perform changes in their own lives, to become active agents in shaping the history that shapes them.

Justice Now

A One-Act Play

Justice Now, a short one-act play, pushes back against those discourses that would marginalize an ethically responsible social justice agenda for qualitative inquiry. The play images a space that celebrates utopian commitments (see Diversi and Moreira, 2009). This space is required if the promises of an international coalition of critical inquiry are to be realized.

Characters:

Speaker One

Speaker Two

Staging Notes: Performers are seated around a seminar table on the third floor of Gregory Hall, a four-story, 125-year-old brick classroom on the campus of the University of Illinois. There are twenty-five chairs along the walls and around a forty-foot long wood table. Two large nature paintings on loan from the art department hang on the north and east walls of the room. There is a pull-down screen at the south end of the room for projecting video. Overhead lights are dimmed. Sun streams in through the two north windows. It is one o'clock in the afternoon. The time is the present. The text of the play is handed from speaker to speaker. The first speaker reads the text for speaker one, the second speaker reads the text for speaker two, and so forth, to the end.

ACT ONE

Scene One: *The Many Ghosts of Paulo Freire*

Speaker One:

The ghosts of Paulo Freire are everywhere. This play is written in and through his language, his words, and his dreams: resisting oppression, critical pedagogy, praxis, freedom, hope, love, decolonizing knowledge, justice, and ethics.

Speaker Two

Reading Paulo Freire has always been for me a vivid experience, an encounter. Since the first time I opened an old, borrowed copy of *La Educación como Práctica de Libertad*, his words spoke to me. The words on a yellowish page, dedicating the book to his parents from whom he learned love and the value of dialogue, created an indelible image in my mind, even before I knew that I wanted to be a teacher. I remember I stayed for a while thinking about those words, my parents, the Latin America of the 1960s—the world in which many Christians understand the radical exigency of love, the world in which my parents fell in love. I was born in 1969, the year Paulo Freire left Chile (Mardones, 2013).

Speaker One:

Paulo taught us that social justice work, like critical pedagogy, takes many different forms: indigenous, queer, critical race, critical social disability, red, black, endarkened, performance, postcolonial, feminist, standpoint, transnational, non-western, Asian, African, It's all tangled up in theory; in decolonizing performances; in indigenous pedagogies and methodologies; in resistance narratives; in clashes between regimes of power, truth, and justice. (Diversi and Moreira, 2009, 28).

Speaker Two:

What does it mean to embrace indigenous pedagogies and methodologies, indigenous poetics?

Speaker One:

We use our bodies and our identities, our colonized experiences to theorize these poetics, pedagogies, and methodologies. Like Gloria Anzaldua we invent our own roots, our own histories, we theorize and live in the spaces between cultures, races, ethnicities, identities, oppressions, and liberations (Diversi, and Moreira, 2009, 23).

Speaker Two:

We need to work through an indigenous politics of critical inquiry. We are in the second Decade of Critical Indigenous Inquiry. In this decade there will be a thoroughgoing transition from discourses about and on method, to discourses centering on power, ethics, and social justice. This discourse will bring new meanings to these terms. It will also involve a rethinking of terms like social justice, democracy, science, and education.

Speaker One:

We want a set of proactive understandings that give indigenous persons increased self-determination and autonomy in their own lives. Individuals should be free to determine their own goals and make sense of their world in terms of culturally meaningful terms. This call for autonomy is not a call for separatism, but rather is an invitation for a dialogue between indigenous and non-indigenous persons. It asks that work done with indigenous persons be initiated by them, benefit them, represent them without prejudice, be legitimated in terms of their key values, and be done by researchers who are accountable for the consequences of their work.

Speaker Two:

This translates into a culturally responsive social justice pedagogy. This pedagogy extends from schools into family, community, into culture and language.

Speaker One:

This involves collaborative storytelling, the co-construction of counter-narratives, and the creation of classrooms as discursive, sacred spaces where indigenous values are experienced. Out of these practices emerge students who are able to exercise self-determination in their own education, students able to achieve their own sense of cultural autonomy and healthy well-being (Bishop, 2005).

Speaker Two:

Culturally responsive pedagogy moves in several directions at
the same time. The classroom obviously becomes one site for
social justice work; clearly there are other sites for social justice
activism.

Speaker One:

Some activists use social justice theatre, and Augusto Boal's
Theatre of the Oppressed to help their students think about
the connection between justice, democracy, and critical inquiry
(Yellow Bird, 2005, 13; also Diversi and Moreira, 2009, 7;
Saldana, 2005).

Scene Two: *Justice, Democracy and Healing*

Speaker One:

Social justice and human rights initiatives involve democracy
and indigenous models of governance. Indigenous models of
democracy involve inclusion and the free and full participation
of all members of a society in civic discourse. The architects
of American democracy subverted this full-inclusion model
when they wrote the U.S. Constitution. They denied citizenship
rights to Native Americans, African Americans, and women.

Speaker Two:

Can colonizer-oppressor and colonized-oppressed ever speak
to one another? Who speaks for whom here? Can there be a
collaboration between oppressed and oppressor?

Speaker One:

It is never straightforward. There is an inevitable tangle
of passion, ignorance, ambivalence, desire and power that
shapes the colonizer-colonized collaborating relationship.
For example, the hyphen that connects Maori and non-Maori
defines a colonial relationship. Each term forces the other into
being. The hyphen can never be erased. There may be, however,
an impulse for indigenous (and non-indigenous) persons to
write from both sides of the hyphen—the outsider-within
(Jones and Jenkins, 2008).

Speaker Two:

Collaborative social justice inquiry can be guided by a set of
ethical principles that include respect, care, equity, empathy,
a commitment to fairness, and a commitment to honoring
indigenous culture and its histories. This is Paulo's pedagogy of
solidarity—this is its promise.

Speaker Two:

It is possible to extend the social justice model to include
justice as healing. This means getting outside the colonizer's
legal cage where "might makes right." It means embedding
justice within a moral community. Legal positivism, a cousin of
epistemological positivism, oppresses indigenous persons. It
has caused great harm and destruction in Native communities
by undermining indigenous concepts of community and
natural law (McCaslin and Breton, 2008).

Speaker One:

Healing is not about fixing persons or getting even. It is about
transforming relationships, about being good relatives and

good neighbors. Healing is spiritual, involving sincere and genuine efforts by all those involved to practice values such as fairness, honesty, compassion, harmony, inclusiveness, trust, humility, openness, and most importantly, respect. This is Paulo's pedagogy of neighborhoods.

Scene Three: Hope, Transformations

Speaker One:

We need a politics of hope. We are the children of Paulo Friere. We believe hope is an ontological need.

Speaker Two:

Hope, faith, and hard work will transform the world. This is a hope grounded in the belief that the demand for basic human rights and the demand for social justice will prevail. But it requires a fight and an investment of great emotion and passion.

Speaker One:

Remember. A pedagogy of hope enacts a politics of resistance and imagines a utopian future. Hope makes radical cultural critique and radical social change possible.

Speaker Two:

But hope alone will not produce change. First there must be pain, and despair. Persons must make pain the object of conscious reflection, the desire to resist, to change. This desire must be wedded to a conscious struggle to change the conditions that create the pain in the first place, (1999, 30–31). Hope makes change possible,

Speaker One:
You can call this Paulo's pedagogy of hope.

The End

References

Bishop, Russell. 2005. Freeing Ourselves from Neo-Colonial Domination in Research: A Kaupapa Maori Approach to Creating Knowledge. In *Handbook of Qualitative Research*, 3rd ed., ed. N. K. Denzin and Yvonna S. Lincoln, 109–138. Thousand Oaks, CA: Sage.

Bloom, Leslie Rebecca, and Patricia Sawin. 2009. Ethical Responsibilities in Feminist Research: Challenging Ourselves to do Activist Research with Women in Poverty. *International Studies of Qualitative Studies in Education* 22 (May–June): 333–351.

Denzin, Norman K. 2010. *The Qualitative Manifesto*. Walnut Creek, CA: Left Coast Press.

Diversi, Marcelo, and Claudio Moreira. 2009. *Betweener Talk: Decolonizing Knowledge Production, Pedagogy, and Praxis*. Walnut Creek, CA: Left Coast Press.

Freire, Paulo. 2005. *Teachers as Cultural Workers: Letters to Those Who Dare Teach*. Trans. Donaldo Macedo, Dale Koeike, and Alexandre Oliveria. Boulder, CO: Westview Press.

Freire, Paulo. 2001. *Pedagogy of the Oppressed*. 30th anniv. ed. Introduced by Donaldo Macedo. New York: Continuum.

Freire, Paulo. 1999. *Pedagogy of Hope*. Trans. Robert R. Barr. New York: Continuum. First published 1992.

Jones, Alison, and Kuni Jenkins. 2008. Rethinking Collaboration: Working the Indigene-Colonizer Hyphen. In *Handbook of Critical and Indigenous Methodologies*, ed. Norman K. Denzin, Yvonna S. Lincoln, and Linda Tuhiwai Smith, 471–486. Thousand Oaks, CA: Sage.

McCaslin, Wanda D., and Denise C. Breton. 2008. Justice as Healing: Going Outside the Colonizer's Cage." In *Handbook of Critical and Indigenous Methodologies*, ed. Norman K. Denzin, Yvonna S. Lincoln, and Linda Tuhiwai Smith, 511–530. Thousand Oaks, CA: Sage.

Mardones, Daninel Johnson. 2013. Forthcoming. Listening to Paulo Freire: Breaking the Silence. *Cultural Studies-Critical Methodologies* 13 (6).

Mertens, Donna M., Heidi M. Holmes, and Raychelle L. Harris. 2009. Transformative Research and Ethics. In *The Handbook of Social Research Ethics*, ed. Donna M. Mertens and Pauline E. Ginsberg, 85–101. Thousand Oaks, CA: Sage.

Mills, C. Wright. 1959. *The Sociological Imagination*. New York: Oxford University Press.

Saldana, Johnny 2005. An Introduction to Ethnodrama. In *Ethnodrama: An Anthology of Reality Theatre*, ed. Johnny Saldana, 1–36. Walnut Creek, CA: AltaMira.

Yellow Bird, Michael. 2005. Tribal Critical Thinking Centers. In *For Indigenous Eyes Only: A Decolonization Handbook*, ed. Waziyatawin Angela Wilson and Michael Yellow Bird, 9–30. Santa Fe, NM: School of American Research.

Notes

1. This essay elaborates arguments in Denzin 2010, 101–114.

Re-imaging Freire Beyond Methods

Donaldo Macedo

Nita Freire and Walter de Oliveira provide readers with a new lens to understand the insightful, critically dialectical, and uncompromisingly democratic themes that characterized Paulo Freire's lifelong quest to imagine, as he often emphasized, a world that is less discriminatory, more just, less dehumanizing, and more humane. In addition, this book could not have been timelier given many liberals and neoliberals' penchant to reduce Freire to a methodology—a process through which his leading ideas toward social justice and liberation are selectively appropriated so as to paralyze his ever-present challenge to educators to engage in praxis. It is only through praxis, not educational practices that infantilize, that one could hope for the transformation of both the social structures that generate human misery and the very actors who construct, shape, and maintain a necrophilic view of history. That is, by relegating Freire's radical democratic ideas to, for example, the dialogical method, these educators attempt to use their association with Freire as a form of progressive mascot while remaining complicit with a neoliberal world view that promotes a fatalistic discourse designed to immobilize history, so that they can accommodate to the status quo—a status quo from which they maintain their privilege and reap benefits and from which they are

Pedagogy of Solidarity, Paulo Freire, Ana Maria Araújo Freire, and Walter de Oliveira. © 2014 by Ana Maria Araújo Freire and Walter Ferreira de Oliveira, pp. 111–117.

able to engage in a social construction of not seeing the evil of a callous capitalism that has given rise to the robber barons of the twenty-first century whose obscene greed is to accumulate a vast store of wealth while the majority of the world's dispossessed, landless, and exploited are routinely relegated to subhuman status.

Freire's leading ideas, such as the relationship between author-ity and freedom, are often watered down by many liberals through a misguided adoption of dialogue-as-method in which the dialectical relations are emptied out and replaced by a bureaucratized dialogical process orchestrated by the facilitator who falsely relinquishes his or her authority as teacher and ends up being a process that gives rise to politics without content. This is what happens a lot with those teachers who confuse authority with authoritarianism and, in their claim to fight authoritarianism, they falsely relinquish their authority as teachers in order to become facilitators, and in the process impose a mechanized dialogical method in a rigid manner that may require, for example, that all students must speak even if they choose not to do so. This rigidity transforms dialogical teaching, not into a search for the object of know-ledge, but into a superficial form of democracy in which all students must forcibly participate in a turn-taking task of "blah-blah-blah." I have had the experience of students suggesting to me that I should monitor the length of time students talk in class in order to ensure equal par-ticipation for all students. In most instances, these suggestions are raised without any concern that the turn-at-talk be related to the as-signed readings. In fact, in many cases, students and their facilitators go to great lengths to over-emphasize the process of turn-taking while de-emphasizing the critical apprehension of the object of knowledge. In the end, their concerns attempt to reduce dialogue to a pure tech-nique. I want to make it clear that in criticizing the mechanization of turn-at-talk, I do not intend to ignore the voices that have been silenced by the inflexible, traditional method of lecturing. What is important to keep in mind is not to develop a pedagogical context whereby the assignment of turn-taking to give voice to students results in a new form of rigid imposition. Instead, it is important to create pedagogical structures that foster critical engagement as the only way for the students to come to voice. The uncritical license to take equal turns speaking in a rigid fashion gives rise to a "blah-blah-blah" dialogue resulting in a form of silencing while speaking. Critical educators should avoid at all costs the blind embracing of approaches that pay lip service to democracy and should always be open to multiple and varied approaches that will enhance the possibility for epistemological curiosity with the object of knowledge. The facile and uncritical acceptance of any methodology regardless of its progressive promise can easily be transformed into a new form of methodological rigidity that constitutes, in my view, a form of methodological terrorism. A vacuous dialogue for conversation only is pernicious to the extent that it de-skills students and facilitators alike by not creating pedagogical spaces for epistemological curiosity, critical consciousness, and agency, which is the only way through which one can transcend valorized experience to embrace new knowledge in order to comprehend one's own experience. In addition, the bureaucratization of the dialogic process not only impedes access to Freire's leading ideas that call for transformation, but it also ignores Freire's repeated renouncement of being a facilitator so as to naively, but not innocently, relinquish the authority of a teacher. As he clearly said, "let me begin responding by categorically saying that I consider myself a teacher and always a teacher. I have never pretended to be a facilitator. What I want to make clear also is in being a teacher, I always teach to facilitate. I cannot accept the notion of a facilitator who facilitates so as not to teach."[1]

This fetish for methods, as Lilia Bartolomé[2] so accurately labeled it, not only goes counter to Freire's proposals for liberation pedagogy, but it also adds to the fragmentation of bodies of knowledge, thus fogging reality and eclipsing the possibility of reading the world critically. In other words, as Nita Freire and Walter de Oliveira forcefully make clear, what is important is the critical engagement with Freire's leading ideas and not the methods for which he is known. What is important is that educators develop the capacity to transcend methods and embrace a humanizing pedagogy as proposed by Freire: "A humanizing education is the path through which men and women can become conscious about their presence in the world—the way they act and think when they develop all of their capacities, taking into consideration their needs, but also the needs and aspirations of others."[3]

A humanizing pedagogy should never be reduced to a process that enables one to hide one's privilege and paternalistically proclaim to want to give the oppressed voice while boasting of one's benevolence—a benevolence that reduces the complex process of coming to voice into a gift package while the grateful recipient of voice is paternalistically turned into trophies and a badge of one's generosity. It is immaterial that the generosity is often false and the posture of giving the oppressed voice smacks of putrid arrogance—an arrogance that allows many liberals to "become enamored and perhaps interested in the [oppressed groups] for a time,"[4] but always shield themselves from the reality that created the oppressive conditions they want to ameliorate in the first place. I am reminded of white colleagues who wear their mentorship of minority students on their sleeves while working aggressively to undermine minority colleagues who have, in fact, come to voice—not as receivers of voice-as-gift, but as an arduous process of *conscientization*. Not only do these white voice givers feel hurt and betrayed by what they perceive as "ungratefulness," they cannot envision themselves outside the role that their privilege has allowed them to cut for themselves as representatives or spokespersons for the oppressed. This overly paternalistic posture is well understood by bell hooks, who characterized the attitude of white feminists as believing that there is "no need to hear your voice when I can talk about you better than you can speak about yourself."[5] This constitutes what could be called a ventriloquist pedagogy, a process through which a subordinated women's experiences are interpreted and recast by white women who claim to want to "give voice" to the voiceless.

Nita Freire and Walter de Oliveira's book, once again, reminds us of Freire's insistence for intellectual coherence—a coherence that narrows the gulf between discourse and action and minimizes contradiction that often paralyzes progressive political projects. In essence, Freire always challenged us to embrace hope as a transformative force by assuming our relationship in the world and with the world as historical agents capable of denouncing any and all forms of oppression, so we can announce a more just and humane world. As he often remarked, "change is difficult but it is possible" and this possibility rests, first and foremost, on our yearning for substantive self-transformation and our ethical posture to follow Gandhi's counsel that "we must be the change we wish to see."[6]

Notes

1. Paulo Freire and Donaldo Macedo, "A Dialogue: Culture, Language, and Race," *Harvard Educational Review* 65, no. 3 (1995): 377–402.
2. Lilia I. Bartolomé, "Beyond the Methods Fetish: Toward a Humanizing Pedagogy" in *Harvard Educational Review* 64, no. 2 (1994): 173–194.
3. Paulo Freire and Frei Betto, *Essa escola chamada vida* (São Paulo: Editora Scipione, 1998), 32.
4. Albert Memmi, *The Colonizer and the Colonized* (Boston: Beacon Press, 1991), 26.
5. bell hooks, *Yearning: Race, Gender and Cultural Politics* (Boston: South End Press, 1990).
6. Quoted in *Time*, February 12, 2007.

Index

activism, hope as, 11
adventure, 90–91
aesthetics, 25
agency
  consumerist view of, 9
  history as foundation of, 11
  hope and, 10
anthropocentrism, 74
Arendt, Hannah, 9, 67
art, education through, 25, 44
authoritarianism
  vs. directivity, 21
  discourse vs. practice, 20
  distinctness of teachers and students
    and, 19
  distortion of P. Freire's ideas concern-
    ing, 92–93
  vs. freedom, 21–22, 94
  recent emergence of, 8–9
  respect for students and, 24
authority/freedom relationship, 7, 10

banking model of education, 30–32, 95
Baudrillard, Jean, 67
Bauman, Zygmunt, 67
becoming. *See* human beings, unfinished
    nature of

beyond, going. *See* directivity
black English, 59–60
Boff, Leonardo, 67
Brugger, Paula, 82

capitalism, modern transformation of,
    8–9
Ceccon, Claudius, 87, 97
charity
  in life of P. Freire, 86
  vs. solidarity, 77, 80
children, historical conceptions of, 17
Christ, 60
Christianity. *See* religion
churches. *See* religion
class divisions, 71, 72
Coelho, Teixeira, 67
colonialism
  multiculturalism and, 60
  profiling and, 63
commodification, 68
community colleges, 81
community spirit, 78–79
confusion, benefits of, 23
constructivism, 27–28
consumerism, 9
contents of education, 19–20

Pedagogy of Solidarity, Paulo Freire, Ana
Maria Araújo Freire, and Walter de Oliveira.
© 2014 by Ana Maria Araújo Freire and
Walter Ferreira de Oliveira, pp. 117–122.

About the Authors

Paulo Freire was one of the major social and educational thinkers of the twentieth century. Prior to his death in 1997, he wrote over twenty books creating and expounding on the idea of critical pedagogy and the methods to implement it, which were widely adopted by progressive educators around the world. More than a scholar, he served as São Paulo's secretary of education, as an advisor on educational reform, and as an agent of social change that had him both jailed and exiled from his native Brazil. His *Pedagogy of the Oppressed* is one of the most influential books in the field of education. Freire was named Patron of Brazilian Education by the national government.

Ana Maria Araújo Freire is a Brazilian educational and social researcher and an activist. She is the widow of Paulo Freire and coauthored several of his later books and organized several volumes about Freire's work.

Walter Fereira de Oliveira is Professor of Public Health at Federal University of Santa Catarina in Brazil.

About the Contributors

Norman K. Denzin is Distinguished Professor of Communication at the University of Illinois, Urbana-Champaign, and a widely published author on cultural criticism, research methodology, and social justice.

Henry A. Giroux holds the Global Television Network Chair in English and Cultural Studies at McMaster University in Canada and is a noted critical educational and cultural theorist.

Donaldo Macedo is Distinguished Professor of Literacy and Education at University of Massachusetts Boston, and is widely published in linguistics, critical literacy, and bilingual and multicultural education.